The Journey of the Mind to God

BONAVENTURE

The Journey of the Mind to God

Translated by
PHILOTHEUS BOEHNER, O.F.M.

Edited, with Introduction and Notes, by
STEPHEN F. BROWN

Hackett Publishing Company
Indianapolis/Cambridge

Bonaventure: 1217–1274

Translation and texts by Philotheus Boehner, O.F.M.
    ©1956 by the Franciscan Institute and
    reprinted 1990.

New materials by Stephen F. Brown
© 1993 by Hackett Publishing Company, Inc.

Printed in the United States of America

25 24 23 22   5 6 7 8

Cover design by Listenberger Design Associates

Text design by Dan Kirklin

For further information please address

    Hackett Publishing Company, Inc.
    P.O. Box 44937
    Indianapolis, Indiana 46244-0937

    www.hackettpublishing.com

Library of Congress Cataloging-in-Publication Data
Bonaventure, Saint, Cardinal, ca. 1217–1274.
    [Itinerarium mentis in Deum. English]
    The Journey of the mind to God/Bonaventure: translated by
    Philotheus Boehner; edited, with introduction and notes, by
Stephen F. Brown
        p.   cm.
Includes bibliographical references.
ISBN 0-87220-201-1 ISBN 0-87220-200-3 (pbk.)
    I. God—Early works to 1800.   2. Mysticism—Catholic Church—Early
works to 1800.   3. Catholic Church—Doctrines.   I. Boehner, Phi-
lotheus.   II. Brown, Stephen F.   III. Title
BT100.B56   1993
248.2'2—dc20   93-24136
                                                            CIP

ISBN-13: 978-0-87220-201-6 (cloth)
ISBN-13: 978-0-87220-200-9 (pbk.)

CONTENTS

CONTENTS

PREFACE

When the editors of Hackett Publishing Company suggested a new handy edition of Saint Bonaventure's *The Journey of the Mind to God* for advanced college courses and graduate seminars, my memory went immediately to the six English translations of the work that already exist. Did we need a seventh?

Certainly there is a need for a new edition. Most are out of print. One is joined with other works of Saint Bonaventure and is quite costly for university and college audiences. A new edition thus seemed appropriate. But was a new translation necessary? I reviewed each of the ones that already existed and came away with great admiration for their accuracy, their readability, or both. After discussing the merits of each with the editors, I decided that the best path would be to follow the translation of Philotheus Boehner, which is still available from the Franciscan Institute at St. Bonaventure University, in its bilingual (Latin-English) form. It stays very close to the Latin in accuracy and is generally quite readable, even lyrical at times. In the translation in this volume I have essentially followed the Boehner English text. A few times I have made corrections, employed less latinized expressions, or searched for a synonym that might better render a technical expression. The changes are few enough that someone who might choose to follow the original Latin in the Boehner bilingual edition would easily be able to discover the alterations I made in my English version.

Another reason for choosing the Boehner edition as the basis for the present volume is the wealth of helpful notes to the text that he provides. Most of these bountiful comments, however, are based on other works of Saint Bonaventure, especially his *Commentary on the Sentences of Peter Lombard*, which only exists in Latin. Thus, most of Boehner's notes are filled with Latin citations that many today would find unhelpful. Our notes are in the vernacular, and even though they are our own translations, we have tried to give references to published English translations when these have existed, so that those who want to read further might do so.

Boehner's introduction was both lengthy and solid. The audience he aimed his remarks at were people he could assume were familiar with Saint Bonaventure, with Saint Francis of Assisi who founded the Franciscan Order to which Saint Bonaventure belonged, and with many other technical aspects of medieval spiritual and intellectual life. Our introduction is aimed more at an audience of upper level university students and professors. The bibliography we have appended to our introduction is also meant to assist them in their further study and research into this Bonaventurean masterwork.

I would like to thank Brother Edward Coughlin, O.F.M., Director of the Franciscan Institute at St. Bonaventure University, for granting permission to use and adapt the Boehner translation and text according to my best judgment. Also I would like to express my gratitude to the Lynde and Harry Bradley Foundation for the generous support they have provided me during the time of my work on this volume. Professor Edward P. Mahoney of Duke University also is owed credit for his advice and kind contributions to my bibliographical entry. A note of gratitude is due, likewise, to Shirley Gee, my Administrative Assistant, for her patience and technical assistance. Finally, I would like to thank my wife, Marie, and my children, Mark and Aimee, for the enthusiastic support they have given me during this endeavor.

Boston College   Stephen F. Brown
July 14, 1993

INTRODUCTION

The Itinerarium or *The Journey of the Mind to God* is one of the great spiritual books of all times. In the past half century it has been translated into English more than a half dozen times. Its greatness, however, lies not only in a certain popular appeal. Its claim to respect is found even more in its deep spiritual message and the challenge it offers to a matter-of-fact view of reality. The author of the work, Saint Bonaventure, never viewed the world in a hard-nosed, factual way. A rose, for him, was always more than a rose. Or, perhaps, we might better say that for Saint Bonaventure a rose, while remaining a rose, tells an attentive viewer a richer story of its reality.

Saint Bonaventure (1217–1274), a professor at the young University of Paris, followed in the spiritual footsteps of Saint Francis of Assisi (1181–1226). Both men saw reality far differently from most of us. Let us look at the two men.

Saint Bonaventure

In the *Itinerarium*, Saint Bonaventure introduces himself as the seventh successor as Minister to the followers of Saint Francis.[1] He became Minister of the Franciscan Order in 1257, at the age of forty. He wrote the *Itinerarium* two years later. This period was a somewhat disturbing time for the early followers of Saint Francis. Already many of them were interpreting the life of the saint and his ideal of poverty in different ways. One group, led by John of Parma, Saint Bonaventure's predecessor as Minister of the Order, challenged the Church's dedication to the poverty of Christ. This group longed for a new age, one predicted by the twelfth-century hermit Joachim of Flora, where the ecclesiastical foundation would be replaced by communities of more spiritual men. Pope Alexander IV saw dangers in this movement. He requested that John of Parma resign as Minister. Bonaventure, elected Minister at the Franciscan Chapter of Rome in 1257, replaced John as a more balanced and disciplined leader.[2]

Bonaventure was a respected Franciscan. Born in the town of Balneoregio, between Orvieto and Viterbo, he received his early education

1 *Itinerarium*, Prologue, 2.

2 Quinn, J. F., "The Chronology of St. Bonaventure (1217–1257)" in *Franciscan Studies* 32 (1972), 168–86.

at the Franciscan friary in his hometown. About 1234, he went to study in the preparatory school for theology, the Arts Faculty at the University of Paris. He entered the Franciscan Order at Paris in 1243 and began his theological studies under Alexander of Hales, the most famous Master of Theology at Paris. Alexander had become a Franciscan shortly before Bonaventure's arrival at the university. Bonaventure also studied with two other renowned Franciscan masters, John of La Rochelle and Odo Rigaud. During his years as an advanced theology student at Paris he lectured on the Bible (1248–1250) and also delivered his commentary on *The Sentences of Peter Lombard* (1250–1252), a text that Alexander of Hales had made an official textbook for the more disciplined doctrinal study of theology at the university. Bonaventure continued to teach theology at Paris until his election as Minister in 1257, as is witnessed by his *Disputed Questions on the Mystery of the Trinity*, his *Disputed Questions on the Knowledge of Christ*, and *The Breviloquium*, all of them university works. Even while Minister to the Franciscan Order, he kept close links to the university. His *Sermons on the Ten Commandments*, *On the Gifts of the Holy Spirit*, and *On the Six Days of Creation*, dating from the late 1260s and early 1270s, were given to University of Paris audiences.[3]

Two points suggested in the preceding paragraphs are important for the understanding of the *Itinerarium*. First of all, Saint Bonaventure's work is heavily laden with symbolic and metaphorical language. In this way, it is very close to the type of language found among the Spiritual Franciscans inspired by Joachim of Flora. Yet, Bonaventure's use of layered language has a certain discipline that rules over, guides, and enriches his symbolism and metaphors. This discipline restrains him from the extreme interpretations found among the Spiritualist writers and the Franciscan brethren who followed their lead. It is this controlled balance that invigorates Bonaventure's work. It is a balance that is achieved to a great extent by his reflection on the writings of Saint Augustine, and particularly by Augustine as he was understood by Bernard of Clairvaux (1090–1153) and Richard of St. Victor (†1173).

The second point to note in reading *The Journey of the Mind to God* is that it has many of the markings of a university sermon.[4] It does not

---

3 Bougerol, G. J., *Introduction to the Works of St. Bonaventure.* Trans. José de Vinck. (Ramsey: Saint Anthony Guild Press, 1964), 37–63.

4 Gilson, E., *Les idées et les lettres.* (Paris: J. Vrin, 1932), 153.

provide an account of an individual's spiritual journey. It is quite technical and a rich catalogue of the myriad signs that might lead those who, like Daniel the prophet and Francis of Assisi, are "men of desire" to the God for Whom their hearts yearn. If you would want to search for the experiences that underlie and inspire Bonaventure's work, you might best find them in *The Confessions* of Saint Augustine. Yet, in the *Itinerarium* of Saint Bonaventure, as in Augustine's own more thematic works, such as *On the Trinity* or *On True Religion*, these experiences have been digested and are presented in terms that might serve as a general guide for others. The *Itinerarium* is not a work describing direct experience. It is a university guidebook and an invitation to a deeper spiritual life. It is a general portrait of how the immediate learning experiences of university students should be understood at their more lasting, deeper, and more tested levels.

If we suggest that to some extent *The Journey of the Mind to God* is a refutation of Spiritualist excesses, Saint Bonaventure does not set himself such a task directly. Rather he achieves this very remote goal by simple exposition and by the balance that informs the work. He does not attempt deliberately to refute Spiritualist visions of Saint Francis's message. He is much more positively focused, and his treatise never descends to polemics. He rather invites us to go back to Augustine's *Confessions*, to his *On the Trinity* and *On True Religion*, to the *On Consideration* of Saint Bernard, to the *Benjamin Maior or Mystical Ark* of Richard of St. Victor, and to the spiritual program of Brother Giles, Francis of Assisi's third follower.[5] Each of these spiritual guides inspired the *Itinerarium*, and it is only within this tradition that we might best discover the more balanced spirituality that informs this work and the message of Saint Francis as Saint Bonaventure understood him.

Saint Francis

Saint Francis, in the tradition of his Order and of the Church, is the "Poor Man of Assisi." For Saint Bonaventure, Francis, as the inspiring force of the *Itinerarium*, is the poor man in whose footsteps he desires to walk. We have said that Saint Bonaventure's work is heavily laden with symbolic and metaphorical language. When he refers to the "poor

5 *Sermon I on Holy Saturday* (*Sabbato sancto. Sermo 1*) (IX, 269). See below in this introduction where we summarize Bonaventure's presentation of the positions of Bernard, Richard, and Giles.

man," what does he mean? While Saint Francis is the inspiration of
Bonaventure's work, it certainly is not because the "Poor Man of Assisi"
was born to economically poor circumstances. Some people are poor
because they are born to poor families. This certainly was not the case
with Saint Francis. His father was a wealthy cloth merchant, and
Francis of Assisi could easily have followed his father's way of life. He
chose to surrender such riches, to pursue a life of voluntary poverty,
a life that imitated Christ, who had no place to lay His head.[6] Like
Christ, Francis was poor in a special sense of the term. He chose to
be poor.

Chosen poverty, though an admirable approach to life, is still not
exactly what Saint Bonaventure views as the key to understanding the
poverty of Francis of Assisi. Bonaventure prefaces Chapter One with
the words: "Here begins the speculation of the poor man in the desert."
Bonaventure's portrait of poverty is not simply a sketch of the nobility
of a life of chosen detachment from material wealth. In Saint Bonaventure's way of appreciating the vocation or calling to the Franciscan
view of the Gospel life, Saint Francis leads us to see a deeper meaning
for the "poor man in the desert." The "poor man in the desert" is one
who recognizes a deeper poverty, the poverty of every creature and
every human being in comparison to the wealth of God's goodness.

Saint Bonaventure, without in any way disdaining the importance of
living according to chosen poverty of means, thus invites his university
audience to consider an even more basic kind of poverty. It is a poverty
inspired by Francis of Assisi, even if Francis never explicitly stated it
in the way that Bonaventure does. This more fundamental poverty is
of great importance, because it makes us aware of a deeper spiritual
impoverishment that cannot be overcome by our own efforts or even by
a chosen life of living poor. As Saint Bonaventure indicates,[7] following a
long tradition, we are bent away from seeking the true riches of God
in a twofold way: our mind by ignorance and our flesh by concupiscence.
For all the virtue that might be found in living a poor life, it is this
other kind of poverty that Bonaventure also wants to draw to our
attention throughout his treatise.

Yet, it is this impoverishment that we cannot remedy on our own.
"Man, blinded and bent over, sits in darkness and does not see the
light of heaven, unless grace comes to his aid—with justice to fight

6 Matthew 8, 20 and Luke 9, 58.
7 *Itinerarium* 1, 7.

concupiscence, and with knowledge and wisdom to oppose ignorance."[8] For Bonaventure, the remedy for our fundamental weakness is manifested in Saint Paul's First Letter to the Corinthians:[9] Christ crucified is the power of God that brings the grace of justice and the grace of knowledge and wisdom. It is the incarnate Word, "full of grace and of truth,"[10] Who offers the grace that rectifies our will and enlightens our mind. With this vision of our basic poverty and its remedy, Bonaventure ends the introductory part of Chapter One with the following directives: "We must first of all pray. Next, we must live holily. Then we must gaze at the spectacles of truth, and by gazing at them, rise step by step until we reach the mountain height where the God of gods is seen on Zion."[11]

For Saint Bonaventure, Francis of Assisi was a man of prayer and a model of a holy life. This much he takes as evident to his audience. But in Chapter Seven, Bonaventure sums up the inspiring role that Francis has played in the speculative exercise he has offered his audience. "He is set forth as an example of perfect contemplation, just as previously he had been of action."[12]

In the Prologue to the work he tells us how Francis became the example of the type of contemplation that fills the main body of *The Journey of the Mind to God*.[13] In 1259 Bonaventure visited Mount Alverno, the place where Saint Francis had received the imprint of Christ's wounds on his body two years before his death. While considering different spiritual ascents to God, he was struck by how the miracle of Saint Francis's stigmata suggested the road to the contemplative heights Francis experienced. It is this road that Bonaventure determined to follow in his treatise.

In his *First Sermon on Holy Saturday*,[14] Bonaventure indicates some of the different spiritual ascents to God that might lead to the peace

---

8 *Ibid.*

9 I Corinthians 1, 30 and 1, 24.

10 John 1, 14 and 1, 17.

11 *Itinerarium* 1, 8.

12 *Itinerarium* 7, 3.

13 *Itinerarium*, Prologue, 2–3.

14 *Sermon I on Holy Saturday* (*Sabbato sancto. Sermo 1*) (IX, 269). On alternative ascents, cf. S. F. Brown. "Reflections on the Structural Sources of Bonaventure's *Itinerarium Mentis in Deum*" in <u>Medieval Philosophy and Modern Times</u>, ed. G. Holmström-Hintikka (The Netherlands, 1997), 1–15.

our hearts seek. There is the path leading to God described by Saint Bernard of Clairvaux in Chapter 14 of his *On Consideration*.[15] This path is pursued through an admiration of God's majesty, a sense of His judgments, a recollection of divine generosity, and an expectation of God's eternal promises.

There is, as an alternative, the road suggested by Richard of St. Victor in Book I of *The Mystical Ark*. There, in Chapter 6, he outlines a sixfold form of contemplation that certainly influenced Bonaventure's *Itinerarium* format. Richard starts with our spontaneous encounter with external things and the wonder they beget. He then passes on to our way of ordering the knowledge we have of sense objects. He views both these levels as mirrors reflecting some awareness of spiritual and divine reality. Then, he moves up to the higher levels of reason. The first rational stage is still attached to imagination. Only as a fourth step do we find reason operating more purely. In his fifth stage Richard's contemplative rises to the level above and beyond reason, and sixthly and finally he climbs to the level, dealing mostly with the Triune God, that not only is above reason but seemingly is opposed to it.[16]

A third form of ascent to God, and one to which Bonaventure gives a great deal of consideration, is the contemplative model provided by Saint Francis's third follower, Giles of Assisi. According to Brother Giles, the soul who wants to attain peace must climb the following steps: 1) he must forget himself and burn with the most ardent desire for union with God; 2) he must be anointed by the consoling balm that is poured on fervent souls by the Holy Spirit to heal the loss he feels for the things he surrendered; 3) he must achieve the kind of ecstasy that abandons the things of sense and turns to God Who is found within; 4) he then must be open to the presence of eternal light through contemplation; 5) he must experience the refreshment that comes from tasting God, like the Israelites, whom Exodus describes with the words: "They beheld God, and they ate and were refreshed";[17]

---

15 *Sancti Bernardi Opera*, t. 3: *Tractatus et opuscula* (edd. J. Leclercq et H. M. Rochais; Rome, 1964), 493.

16 Richardus de Sancto Victore, *Benjamin Maior*, III, 6 (PL 196, 116–17). On the Trinitarian perspective of Richard of St. Victor and how it follows St. Augustine and differs from St. Bonaventure, see Zachary Hayes's introduction to Saint Bonaventure, *Disputed Questions on the Mystery of the Trinity* (St. Bonaventure, N.Y., 1979), 13–24.

17 Exodus 24, 11.

6) he must embrace God; 7) and then the sabbath rest will be given to him and he will sleep in the arms of the Lord.[18]

Bonaventure's meditation on the stigmata of Saint Francis inspired him with a model that borrows elements from each of these three alternatives and yet provides particular characteristics that make it a distinct path to the peace that only God can give. As Bonaventure reminds us,[19] Francis's vision was that of a crucified six-winged seraph. His stigmata or the imprinting of the wounds of the Crucified on his body showed Francis's union with Christ. Even more literally he could say with Saint Paul: "With Christ I am nailed to the Cross. It is now no longer I that live, but Christ lives in me."[20] In its own way Bonaventure's *Itinerarium* is meant to lead our minds to a similar union with God. Each of the six steps—parallel to the six wings of the Seraph—is his attempt to reveal to us more and more fully God's union with the "men of desire." Under Bonaventure's tutelage, with each step we are made more and more aware of God's presence in all that we know. Inspired by Francis of Assisi's vision, Bonaventure sees that it is Christ Who enkindles this desire in us by the white flame of His most burning Passion. We gain in the riches of God as we die to our own cares and concerns. The crucified Christ and the "crucified" Francis have taught Bonaventure to pray, as he does in the last paragraph[21] of his work: "Let us, then, die and enter into this darkness. Let us silence all our cares, our desires, and our imaginings. With Christ crucified, let us pass out of this world to the Father, so that when the Father is shown to us, we may . . . rejoice with David, saying: My flesh and my heart have fainted away: You are the God of my heart, and the God that is my portion forever."

The Plan of the *Itinerarium*

The work is divided into the prologue and seven chapters. The prologue introduces us to the prayerful spirit required to begin our journey on the road to peace. It also anticipates the six steps toward union with God that the *Itinerarium* will indicate to us. Furthermore, it underscores

---

18 *Sermon I on Holy Saturday* (*Sabbato sancto. Sermo 1*) (IX, 269).

19 *Itinerarium*, Prologue, 3.

20 II Corinthians 12, 2; Galatians 2, 20.

21 *Itinerarium*, 7, 6.

the need for justice or a holy life to begin the climb toward this goal with the words: "The mirror of the external world . . . is of little or no avail unless the mirror of our soul has been cleansed and polished."[22]

Chapter One is split into two parts: an introductory section and then a description of the first step of the ladder on the journey of the mind to God. The introductory section outlines the six steps marking this journey and once again stresses the need for prayer and a holy life.

A. The first two steps deal with the vestiges
   of God in the visible world.

The first step completes Chapter One and focuses on the external world. Because bent-over man's vision is distorted by ignorance and concupiscence, he fails to see sense realities as he should. The sacred Scriptures bring man back to a true vision of sensible reality by revealing that these objects of our sense experience do not explain themselves. The soul enlightened by the Scriptural message and the true description of their reality sees that they are created by God through His benevolence and fit into His most wise plan. If, like Hugh of Saint Victor in his *Didascalicon*,[23] we looked at their origin, their greatness, their multitude, their beauty, their plenitude, their activity, and their order, then we would realize that if we do not see God's power, wisdom, and goodness in the splendor of created things, then we are blind.

The second step brings us to even greater heights in regard to sensible things. The first step focused on the origin, greatness, beauty, and other characteristics of external objects and used these things as mirrors reflecting the power, wisdom, and goodness of God. We were led *through* them to God above Who in His goodness has created them according to His wise purposes. The second step centers on the presence of God *in* things. This stage is akin to the message of Saint Paul to the Athenians: "In Him we live and move and have our being."[24] Our sense knowledge, enjoyment, and judgments tell us that God's essence, power, and presence are in visible creation. This approach to visible things shows the strong influence of Saint Augustine's philosophy, and especially of his illumination theory of knowledge. According

22 *Itinerarium*, Prologue, 4.
23 Hugo de Sancto Victore, *Didascalicon*, VII, 1–12 (PL 176, 811–21).
24 Acts 17, 28.

to Augustine and Bonaventure, the first thing we know is God, even though we are not aware of this at first. Just as we would not see the colors and shapes of a stained-glass window unless the invisible sun was illuminating them, so we would not see visible things if the invisible God was not illuminating them from within. God, then, is present in things, and if we analyze our sense knowledge, our enjoyment of sense objects, and the judgments we make concerning them, we would come to realize God's invisible presence in them. Bonaventure does this in Chapter Two.

B. The third and fourth steps deal with the image of God in the mind.

In *the third step* the soul turns from the consideration of visible objects to itself as the image of God. It sees that it loves itself, and yet could not do so unless it knew itself. Neither could it know itself unless it summoned itself to conscious memory. As for Saint Augustine in *On the Trinity*, so for Saint Bonaventure in Chapter Three it is *through* memory, intelligence, and will as the three faculties of the one soul that we discover the most suitable analogy in the natural order to the three Persons in the one God.

The fourth step, in a way parallel to the second step, leads to a consideration of the presence of God *in* the soul. God's presence in the soul by grace restores it from its bent-over form to its supernatural likeness or similitude to God. The entire beauty of the soul is displayed in Chapter Four, as it unfolds its supernatural riches by putting on the theological virtues of faith, hope, and love, regaining its spiritual senses, and becoming purified, enlightened, and perfected.

C. The fifth and sixth steps move above the mind to the essential and personal attributes of God.

The fifth step builds on observations made at earlier stages. In discussing at the second step the priority of our knowledge of God, for example, we discovered that, even though we were not aware of it, a full analysis reveals that God is the first thing known. Since all things we know are beings, then God as the primary thing known must be Being in its fullest sense. Chapter Five takes its lead from John of Damascus,[25]

25 John of Damascus, *On the Orthodox Faith*, I, 9, 142 (PG 94, 835–36). Cf. Exodus 3, 14.

who tells us "that of all the names predicated of God the more proper name is 'He Who Is,' since when God spoke to Moses on the mountain, He said: Say to the children of Israel 'He Who Is' has sent me." This chapter thus raises our minds to a consideration of that Being Who is called pure being and simple being and absolute being, that is, the first Being Who is most simple, most actual, most perfect, and supremely one.

The sixth step develops the realization that Being also is The Good. Pseudo-Dionysius,[26] one of the strong influences on Saint Bonaventure in this work, considered 'The Good' the perfect name for God, since it best manifests that God though one is not solitary. The Good is self-communicating love. The mind reaches its highest perfection in contemplating the communicative life of the triune God, and especially in contemplating God's Son, Christ, the perfect image of the invisible God.

The soul has climbed the six-story mountain. The mind has reached the high point of its being. The intellect has done all that it can do to bring itself to the fullest possible understanding of God, the object of the soul's desire. The mind not only yearns to understand God; it yearns to be united with Him. Who can help it bridge the gulf that separates it from the Beloved? Chapter Seven tells us that there is one being who can serve as the Mediator, Jesus Christ. As the Crucified He came to Saint Francis and transformed him to His image. Upon the Crucified now the soul must fix its gaze and wait, full of confidence in Christ, expecting from His grace the ultimate union with God.

---

26 Pseudo-Dionysius, *On the Divine Names*, III, 1 (PG 3, 679–80).

BIBLIOGRAPHY

I. Works of Saint Bonaventure:

A. Latin:

Doctoris Seraphici S. Bonaventurae *Opera omnia. ed. studio et cura Patrum Collegii a S. Bonaventura ad plurimos codices mss. emendata, anecdotis aucta, prolegomenis scholiis notisque illustrata*, Quaracchi, 1882–1902, 10 volumes.

Tom. I.   *Commentarium in Librum Primum Sententiarum.*
Tom. II.   *Commentarium in Librum Secundum Sententiarum.*
Tom. III. *Commentarium in Librum Tertium Sententiarum.*
Tom. IV. *Commentarium in Librum Quartum Sententiarum.*
Tom. V.   *Opuscula varia theologica.*
Tom. VI. *Commentarium in Sacram Scripturam.*
Tom. VII. *Commentarium in evangelium S. Lucae.*
Tom. VIII. *Opuscula varia ad theologicam mysticam et res ordinis fratrum minorum spectantia.*
Tom. IX. *Sermones de tempore, de sanctis, de B. Virgine Maria et de diversis.*
Tom. X.   *Operum omnium complementum.*

B. Translations:

1. a. *De reductione artium ad theologiam.* A commentary with an introduction and English translation by Sr. Emma Thérèse Healy. St. Bonaventure, N.Y., 1955.

   b. *On Retracing the Arts to Theology* (in *The Works of Bonaventure*, vol. 3). Translated into English by José de Vinck. Paterson, N.J., 1966.

2. a. *The Franciscan Vision.* English translation and introduction by James O'Mahoney. London, 1937.

   b. *Saint Bonaventura: The Mind's Road to God.* Translated into English with an introduction by George Boas. Indianapolis, Ind., 1953.

   c. *Itinerarium mentis in Deum.* With an introduction, English translation, and commentary by Philotheus Boehner. St. Bonaventure, N.Y., 1956.

   d. *The Journey of the Mind to God* in *St. Bonaventure: Mystical Opuscula.* Translated into English by José de Vinck. Paterson, N.J., 1960.

   e. *The Soul's Journey into God* in *Bonaventure.* Translated into English by Ewert Cousins. New York, Ramsey, Toronto, 1978.

   f. *The Mind's Journey to God.* Translated into English by Lawrence S. Cunningham. Chicago, 1979.

   g. *Bonaventura, Itinerarium mentis in Deum* und *De reductione artium ad theologiam.* Introduction, German translation, and notes by J. Kaup. Munich, 1961.

h. *S. Bonaventura, Itinerario delle mente verso Dio*. With introduction, Italian translation, and notes by C. Ottaviano. Palermo, 1933.

i. *Saint Bonaventure, Itineraire de l'esprit vers Dieu*. With introduction, French translation, and notes by Henri Dumèry. Paris, 1960.

3. *The Works of Bonaventure*, 5 volumes. Translated by José de Vinck. Paterson, N.J., 1960–1970.

   a. *Mystical Opuscula*: i) *The Journey of the Mind to God*; ii) *The Triple Way*; iii) *The Tree of Life*; iv) *The Mystical Vine*; v) *On the Perfection of Life, Addressed to Sisters*, 1960.

   b. *The Breviloquium*, 1963.

   c. *Opuscula—Second Series*: i) *Praise of the Holy Cross*; ii) *On Retracing the Arts to Theology*; iii) *Soliloquy on the Four Spiritual Exercises*; iv) *The Six Wings of the Seraph*; v) *On the Five Feasts of the Child Jesus*; vi) *On How to Prepare for the Celebration of Mass*; vii) *On the Government of the Soul*; viii) *Letter Containing Twenty-five Points to Remember*, 1966.

   d. *Defense of the Mendicants*, 1966.

   e. *Collations on the Six Days*, 1970.

4. *Bonaventure: The Soul's Journey into God, The Tree of Life, The Life of St. Francis*. A translation and introduction by Ewert Cousins. New York, Ramsey, Toronto, 1978.

5. *Major and Minor Life of St. Francis*, with excerpts from other works of St. Bonaventure. Translated by Benen Fahy in *St. Francis of Assisi: Writings and Early Biographies, English Omnibus of the Sources for the Life of St. Francis*. Edited by Marion A. Habig. Chicago, 1974, 627–851.

6. *Rooted in Faith: Homilies to a Contemporary World by St. Bonaventure*. Translated with an introductory essay by Merigwen Schumacher. Chicago, 1974.

7. *What Manner of Man? Sermons on Christ by St. Bonaventure*. Translated with introduction and commentary by Zachary Hayes. Chicago, 1974.

8. *Disputed Questions on the Mystery of the Trinity*. Translated with an introduction and commentary by Zachary Hayes. St. Bonaventure, N.Y., 1979.

9. *St. Bonaventure as a Biblical Commentator*. A translation and analysis of his *Commentary on Luke 18, 34–19, 42* by Thomas Reist. Lanham, Md., 1985.

10. *Disputed Questions Concerning Christ's Knowledge*, q. 4 in *A Scholastic Miscellany*. Edited by Eugene Fairweather. Philadelphia, 1956, 379–401.

11. *On the Eternity of the World* (Thomas Aquinas, Siger of Brabant, and St. Bonaventure). Translation by C. Vollert, L. H. Kendzierski, and Paul M. Byrne. Milwaukee, 1964.

II. Bibliography:

Bibliographia Bonaventuriana (c. 1850–1973), cura J. G. Bougerol in Vol. V of *San Bonaventura 1274–1974*. Edited by J. G. Bougerol. Grottaferrata, 1974.

III. Secondary Sources:

Allard, G. H., "La technique de la 'reductio' chez Bonaventure," in *San Bonaventura*, II, 395–416.

Andres, F., "Die Stufen der *Contemplatio* in Bonaventuras *Itinerarium mentis in Deum* und im *Beniamin minor* des Richard von St. Viktor," in *Franziskanische Studien* 7 (1921), 189–200.

Berg, L., "Die Analogielehre des heiligen Bonaventura," in *Studium Generale* 8 (1955), 662–70.

Bernath, K., "*Mensura fidei*. Zahlen und Zahlenverhältnis bei Bonaventura," in *Miscellanea Mediaevalia* 16/1 (1983), 65–85.

Bérubé, C., *De la philosophie à la sagesse chez Saint Bonaventure et Roger Bacon* (*Bibliotheca Seraphico—Capuccina*, v. 26). Rome, 1976.

———, "De la théologie de l'image à la philosophie de l'objet de l'intelligence chez Saint Bonaventure," in *San Bonaventura*, III, 161–200.

———, "Grandeur et misère de notre connaissance de Dieu chez Saint Bonaventure," in *Doctor Seraphicus* 27 (1980), 51–81.

Bettoni, E., *Il problema della conoscibilita de Dio nella scuola francescana: Alessandro d'Hales, S. Bonaventura, Duns Scoto*. Padua, 1950.

———, *St. Bonaventure*. Tr. Angelus Gambatese (Notre Dame, 1964).

Beumer, J., "Zwei schwierige Begriffe in der mystischen Theologie Bonaventuras ('*raptus*' und '*ecstasis*')," in *Franziskanische Studien* 56 (1974), 249–62.

Bissen, J.-M., "De la contemplation," in *Etudes franciscaines* 42 (1930), 5–17.

———, "Les conditions de la contemplation selon saint Bonaventure," in *La France franciscaine* 17 (1934), 387–404.

———, "La contemplation selon saint Bonaventure" in *La France franciscaine* 14 (1931), 175–92.

———, "Les degrés de la contemplation selon saint Bonaventure," in *La France franciscaine* 14 (1931), 439–64, and 15 (1932), 87–105.

———, "Les effets de la contemplation selon saint Bonaventure," in *La France franciscaine* 19 (1936), 20–29.

———, *L'exemplarisme divin selon Saint Bonaventure*. (Etudes de philosophie médiévale 9). Paris, 1929.

———, "L'importance de la contemplation selon saint Bonaventure," in *La France franciscaine* 15 (1932), 437–54.

Bonaventure and Aquinas: Enduring Philosophers. Edited by R. W. Shahan and F. J. Kovach. Norman, 1976.

Bonnefoy, J. F., *Le Saint Esprit et ses dons selon saint Bonaventure*. Paris: J. Vrin, 1929.

Bougerol, J. G., *Introduction to the Works of Bonaventure*. Translation by José de Vinck. Paterson, N.J., 1964.

————, "Saint Bonaventure et Aristote," in *Archives d'Histoire doctrinale et littéraire du Moyen Age* 49 (1973), 135–222.

————, *Saint Bonaventure: Etudes sur les sources de sa pensée*. Aldershot, 1989.

————, *Saint Bonaventure: un maître de sagesse*. Paris, 1966.

Brady, I. C., "The Authenticity of Two Sermons of St. Bonaventure," in *Franciscan Studies* 28 (1968), 4–26.

Chatillon, J., "Saint Bonaventure et la philosophie," in *San Bonaventura*, I, 429–46.

Cousins, E. H., *Bonaventure and the Coincidence of Opposites*. Chicago, 1978.

————, "Bonaventure and the Coincidence of Opposites: A Response to Critics," in *Theological Studies* 42 (1981), 277–90.

————, "Bonaventure, the Coincidence of Opposites and Nicholas of Cusa," in *Studies Honoring Ignatius Charles Brady, Friar Minor*. Edited by Romano S. Almagno and Conrad L. Harkins. St. Bonaventure, N.Y., 1976, 177–97.

————, "Language as Metaphysics in Bonaventure," in *Miscellanea Mediaevalia* 13/2 (1981), 946–51.

————, "St. Bonaventure, St. Thomas and the Movement of Thought in the 13th Century," in *Bonaventure and Aquinas: Enduring Philosophers*, 5–23.

————, "The Coincidence of Opposites in the Christology of St. Bonaventure," in *Franciscan Studies* 28 (1968), 27–46.

————, "The Two Poles of St. Bonaventure's Theology," in *San Bonaventura*, IV, 153–76.

Crowley, T., "Illumination and Certitude" in *San Bonaventura*, III, 431–48.

Dady, M. R., *The Theory of Knowledge of St. Bonaventure*. Washington, D.C., 1939.

Dettloff, W., "Christus tenens medium in omnibus," in *Wissenschaft und Weisheit* 20 (1957), 28–42.

————, "Die franziskanische Theologie des hl. Bonaventura," in *San Bonaventura*, I, 495–512.

————, "Die franziskanische Vorentscheidung im theologischen Denken des heiligen Bonaventura," in *Münchener Theologische Zeitschrift* 13 (1962), 107–15.

————, "Die Geistigkeit des Hl. Franziskus in der Theologie der Franziskaner," in *Wissenschaft und Weisheit* 19 (1956), 197–211.

————, "Himmlische und kirchliche Hierarchie bei Bonaventura," in *Miscellanaea Mediaevalia* 12/1 (1979), 41–55.

Doucet, V., "De naturali seu innato supernaturali beatitudinis desiderio," in *Antonianum* 4 (1929), 167–208.

Elsasser, A., *Christus, der Lehrer des Sittlichen: Die Christologischen Grundlagen für die Erkenntnis des Sittlichen nach der Lehre Bonaventuras*. Munich, 1968.

Emery, Kent Jr., "Denys the Carthusian and the Doxography of Scholastic Theology," in *Ad Litteram: Authoritative Texts and Their Medieval Readers.* Notre Dame, 1992, 327–59.

Engemann, A. "Erleuchtungslehre als *Resolutio* und *Reductio* nach Bonaventura," in *Wissenschaft und Weisheit* 1 (1934), 211–42.

Ennis, H., "The Primacy of the Virtue of Charity in Morality According to Saint Bonaventure," in *Antonianum* 50 (1975), 418–56.

Fischer, K., *De Deo trino et uno. Das Verhältnis von productio und reductio in seiner Bedeutung für die Gotteslehre Bonaventuras.* (Forschungen zur systematischen und ökumenischen Theologie 38). Göttingen, 1978.

Fleming, J. V., *An Introduction to the Franciscan Literature of the Middle Ages.* Chicago: Franciscan Herald Press, 1977.

Foschee, C. N., "St. Bonaventure and the Augustinian Concept of *Mens*," in *Franciscan Studies* 27 (1967), 163–75.

Gendreau, B. A., "The Quest for Certainty in Bonaventure," in *Franciscan Studies* 21 (1961), 104–227.

Gerken, A., "Bonaventuras Konvenienzgründe für die Inkarnation des Sohnes," in *Wissenschaft und Weisheit,* 23 (1960), 131–46.

———, "Der johanneische Ansatz in der Christologie des hl. Bonaventura," in *Wissenschaft und Weisheit,* 27 (1964), 89–102.

———, "Das Verhältnis von Schöpfungs- und Erlösungsordnung im '*Itinerarium mentis in Deum*' des hl. Bonaventura," in *San Bonaventura,* IV, 283–310.

———, *Theologie des Wortes. Das Verhältnis von Schöpfung und Inkarnation bei Bonaventura.* Düsseldorf, 1963.

Gilson, E., *The Christian Philosophy of St. Bonaventure.* Tr. Dom Illtyd Trethowan and Frank J. Sheed. Paterson, N.J., 1965.

Grünewald, S., "Zur Mystik des heiligen Bonaventuras," in *Zeitschrift für Aszese und Mystik* 9 (1934), 124–32 and 219–32.

Guardini, R., *Systembildende Elemente in der Theologie Bonaventuras. Die Lehre vom Lumen mentis, von der Gradatio entium und der Influentia sensus et motus.* Edited by Werner Dettloff; Leiden, 1964.

Hamesse, J., "Le concept 'ordo' dans quelques oeuvres de Saint Bonaventure," in *Lessico Intellettuale Europeo XX: Ordo.* Rome, 1977, 27–57.

Hayes, Z., "Christology and Metaphysics in the Thought of Bonaventure," in *Journal of Religion* 58 (1978), suppl., 82–96.

———, "Incarnation and Creation in the Theology of Saint Bonaventure," in *Studies Honoring Ignatius Charles Brady, Friar Minor.* Edited by Romano S. Almagno and Conrad L. Harkins; St. Bonaventure, N.Y., 1976, 309–30.

———, "The Meaning of *Convenientia* in the Metaphysics of St. Bonaventure," in *Franciscan Studies,* 12 (1974), 74–100.

———, *What Manner of Man. Sermons on Christ by St. Bonaventure.* Translation, with introduction and commentary. Chicago, 1974.

Heinz, H., *Trinitarische Begegnungen bei Bonaventura. Fruchtbarkeit einer appropri-*

ativen Trinitäts-theologie. (*Beiträge zur Geschichte der Philosophie und Theologie des Mittelalters*, N.F. 18). Münster, 1985.

Hellmann, J.A.W., *Ordo—Untersuchungen eines Grundgedankens in der Theologie Bonaventuras.* (Veröffentlichungen des Grabmann-Instituts, N.F. 18). Munich, 1974.

Hinwood, B., "The Principles Underlying Saint Bonaventure's Division of Human Knowledge," in *San Bonaventura*, III, 471–504.

————, "The Division of Human Knowledge in the Writings of Saint Bonaventure," in *Franciscan Studies*, 38 (1978), 220–59.

Hödl, L., "'Gott-schauen' im theologischen Verständnis des hl. Bonaventura," in *Franziskanische Studien* 56 (1974), 165–78.

Hülsbusch, W., *Elemente einer Kreuzestheologie in den Spätschriften Bonaventuras.* Düsseldorf, 1968.

Javelet, R., "Réflexions sur l'Exemplarisme bonaventurien," in *San Bonaventura*, IV, 349–70.

Kuntz, Paul G., and Marion L. Kuntz, *Jacob's Ladder and the Tree of Life: Concepts of Hierarchy and the Great Chain of Being.* New York, 1987.

Landsberg, P. L. "La philosophie de l'experience mystique: *L'Itinerarium*," in *La Vie spirituelle* 51 (1937), 71–85.

Lang, Helen S., "Bonaventure's Delight in Sensation," in *New Scholasticism* 60 (1986), 72–90.

Lazzarini, R., *S. Bonaventura. Filosofo e mystico del Cristianesimo.* Milan, 1946.

Lexique Saint Bonaventure. (Ed. J. G. Bougerol, Paris, 1969).

Longpré, E., "Bonaventure, saint," *Dictionnaire de spiritualité* (Paris, 1937), 1, 1768–1843.

————, "La théologie mystique de saint Bonaventure," in *Archivum Franciscanum Historicum* 14 (1921), 263–99.

Luyckz, B. A., *Die Erkenntnislehre Bonaventuras.* (*Beiträge der Geschichte der Philosophie und Theologie des Mittelalters*, XXIII, 3–4). Münster, 1923.

Mahoney, Edward P., "The Metaphysical Foundations of the Hierarchy of Being According to Some Late Medieval and Renaissance Philosophers," in *Philosophies of Existence, Ancient and Medieval.* New York, 1982, 165–257.

Majchrzak, Colman J., *A Brief History of Bonaventurianism.* Pulaski, Wis., 1957.

McAndrew, P. J., "Theory of Divine Illumination in St. Bonaventure," in *The New Scholasticism* 6 (1932), 32–50.

McEvoy, J., "Microcosm and Macrocosm in the Writings of St. Bonaventure," in *San Bonaventura*, II, 309–43.

McGinn, B., "Ascension and Introversion in the *Itinerarium mentis in Deum*," in *San Bonaventura*, III, 535–52.

————, "The Significance of Bonaventure's Theology of History," in *Journal of Religion* 58 (1978), suppl., 64–81.

Mercker, H. J., *Schriftauslegung als Weltauslegung: Untersuchungen zur Stellung der Schrift in der Theologie Bonaventuras.* (Veröffentlichungen des Grabmann-Institutes, N.F. 15). Munich, 1971.

Moorman, J., *A History of the Franciscan Order: From Its Origins to the Year 1517.* Oxford, 1968.

Mulligan, R. W., *"Portio superior* and *portio inferior rationis* in the Writings of St. Bonaventure," in *Franciscan Studies* 15 (1955), 332–49.

Nemetz, A., "What St. Bonaventure Has Given to Philosophers Today," in *Franciscan Studies*, 19 (1959), 1–12.

O'Donnell, J., *The Psychology of St. Bonaventure and St. Thomas Aquinas.* Washington, D.C., 1937.

Platzech, E. W., "Die Verwendung der 'via Anselmiana' bei Bonaventura," in *Analecta Anselmiana* IV/1 (1975), 127–45.

Prentice, R., *The Concept of Love According to St. Bonaventure.* St. Bonaventure, N.Y., 1949.

Quinn, J. F., "Certitude of Reason and Faith in St. Bonaventure and St. Thomas," in *St. Thomas Aquinas 1274–1974, Commemorative Studies.* Toronto, 1974; II, 105–40.

———, "The Chronology of Saint Bonaventure (1217–1257)," in *Franciscan Studies* 32 (1972), 168–86.

———, *The Historical Constitution of St. Bonaventure's Philosophy.* (Pontifical Institute of Mediaeval Studies, Studies and Texts 23). Toronto, 1973.

———, "The Role of the Holy Spirit in St. Bonaventure's Theology," in *Franciscan Studies* 33 (1973), 273–84.

———, "The *scientia sermocinalis* of St. Bonaventure and His Use of Language Regarding the Mystery of the Trinity," in *Miscellanea Mediaevalia* 13/1 (1981), 413–23.

Rahner, Karl, "Der Begriff der Ecstasis bei Bonaventura," in *Zeitschrift für Aszese und Mystik* 9 (1934), 1–19.

———, "Doctrine of the Spiritual Senses in the Middle Ages," in *Theological Investigations* 16, 104–34.

———, "La doctrine des sens spirituels au Moyen Age, en particulier chez saint Bonaventure," in *Revue d'ascétique et de mystique* 14 (1933), 263–99.

Ratzinger, J., *The Theology of History in St. Bonaventure.* Translated by Zachary Hayes. Chicago, 1971.

Rauch, W., *Das Buch Gottes, eine systematische Untersuchung des Buchbegriffes bei Bonaventura.* Munich, 1961.

Rosenmöller, B., *Religiöse Erkenntnis nach Bonaventura.* (*Beiträge zur Geschichte der Philosophie und Theologie der Mittelalters*, XXV, 3–4). Münster, 1924.

Russo, R., *La metodologia del sapere nel sermone di S. Bonaventura "Unus est magister vester Christus."* Grottaferrata, 1982.

S. Bonaventure 1274–1974. Volumen commemorativum anni septies centenarii a morte S. Bonaventurae Doctoris Seraphici. Edited by J. G. Bougerol et al. Grottaferrata, 1973.

San Bonaventura—Maestro di vita francescana e di sapieza christiana. (*Atti del Congresso internazionale per il VII centenario di San Bonaventura da Bognoregio,* 5 vols.) Edited by A. Pompei. Rome, 1974).

Sauer, E. *Die religiöse Wertung der Welt in Bonaventuras Itinerarium mentis in Deum.* (Franzikanische Forschungen 4). Werl, 1937.

Schachten, W., *Intellectus Verbi. Die Erkenntnis im Mitvollzug des Wortes nach Bonaventura.* (Symposion 44). Freiburg, 1973.

————, "Die Trinitätslehre Bonaventuras als Explikation der Offenbarung vom personalem Gott," in *Franziskanische Studien* 56 (1974), 191–214.

Schaefer, A., "The Position and Function of Man in the Created World According to Saint Bonaventure," in *Franciscan Studies* 20 (1960), 261–316, and 21 (1961), 233–82.

Schmaus, M. "Die Trinitätskonzeption in Bonaventuras *Itinerarium mentis in Deum,*" in *Wissenschaft und Weltbild* 15 (1962), 229–37.

Schulte, H., "Gotteserkenntnis und 'conversio' bei Bonaventura," in *Theologie und Philosophie* 49 (1974), 181–98.

Schwendinger, F., "Die Erkenntnis in den ewigen Ideen nach der Lehre des hl. Bonaventura," in *Franziskanische Studien* 15 (1928), 69–95, and 16 (1929), 29–64.

Sépinski, A., *La psychologie du Christ chez Saint Bonaventure.* Paris, 1948.

Spargo, E.J.M., *The Category of the Aesthetic in the Philosophy of Saint Bonaventure.* (Franciscan Institute Publications, 11). St. Bonaventure, N.Y., 1953.

Speer, A., *Triplex Veritas: Wahrheitsverständnis und philosophische Denkform Bonaventuras.* (Franziskanische Forschungen 32). Werl, 1987.

Stohr, A., *Die Trinitätslehre des hl. Bonaventura.* Münster, 1923.

Szabó, T., *De SS. Trinitate in creaturis refulgente doctrina S. Bonaventurae.* Rome, 1955.

Tavard, G. H., "The Coincidence of Opposites: A Recent Interpretation of Bonaventure," in *Theological Studies* 41 (1980), 576–84.

————, *Transiency and Permanence. The Nature of Theology according to St. Bonaventure.* Saint Bonaventure, N.Y., 1954.

Turney, L., *The Symbolism of the Temple in St. Bonaventure's "Itinerarium mentis in Deum,"* (Ph.D. Dissertation, Fordham University, 1968).

Vanni Rovighi, S., *San Bonaventura.* Milan, 1974.

Veuthy, L., *La filosofia Cristiana di San Bonaventura.* Rome, 1971.

Vignaux, P., "Condition historique de la pensée de Saint Bonaventure: Christocentrisme, eschatologie et situation de la culture philosophique," in *San Bonaventura,* I, 409–27.

Wéber, E.-H., *Dialogue et dissensions entre Saint Bonaventure et Saint Thomas d'Aquin à Paris (1252-1273).* (Bibliothèque Thomiste XLI). Paris, 1974.

Welte, B., "Die Zahl als göttliche Spur. Eine Bonaventura-Interpretation" in Welte, B. (ed.), *Auf der Spur des Ewigen.* Freiburg, 1965, 49–61.

Wenin, C., "La connaissance philosophique d'après Saint Bonaventure" in *L'homme et son destin.* (Actes du premier Congrès international de Philosophie médiévale). Louvain, 1960, 485–94.

Zigrossi, A., *Saggio sul Neoplatonismo di S. Bonaventura.* Florence, 1954.

THE JOURNEY OF THE MIND TO GOD

PROLOGUE

1. In the beginning I call upon the very first Beginning[1] from Whom all enlightenment flows, the *Father of Lights*,[2] from Whom is *every best and perfect gift*,[3] that is upon the Eternal Father, through His Son, our Lord Jesus Christ, that, through the intercession of the most Blessed Virgin Mary, Mother of that same God and our Lord Jesus Christ, and through that of blessed Francis, our guide and father, *He may enlighten the eyes of our mind to guide our feet into the way of* that *peace which surpasses all understanding*,[4] that peace which our Lord Jesus Christ preached to us and which He gave to us. His message of peace[5] our father Francis ever repeated, announcing 'Peace' at the beginning and at the end of all his sermons,[6] making every greeting a wish for peace, making every prayer a sigh for ecstatic peace, like a citizen of that Jerusalem, about which the Man of Peace, *who was peaceable with those that hated peace*, exhorts us concerning it: *Pray for the things that are to the peace of Jerusalem.* For He knew indeed that only in peace was the throne of Solomon established, as it is written: *In peace is his place and his abode is in Zion.*[7]

2. Inspired by the example of our blessed father, Francis, I wanted to seek after this peace with yearning soul, sinner that I am and all unworthy, yet seventh successor as Minister to all the brethren in the place of the blessed father after his death; it happened that, thirty-three years after the death of the Saint,[8] about the time of his passing, moved by a divine impulse, I withdrew to Mount Alverno, as to a place of quiet, there to satisfy the yearning of my soul for peace. While I dwelt there, pondering on certain spiritual ascents to God, I was struck, among other things, by that miracle which in this very place had happened to the blessed Francis, that is, the vision he received of the winged seraph in the form of the Crucified. As I reflected on this marvel, it immediately seemed to me that this vision might suggest the rising of Saint Francis into contemplation and point out the way by which that state of contemplation may be reached.

3. The six wings of the seraph can be rightly understood as signifying the six progressive illuminations by which the soul is disposed, as by certain grades or steps, to pass over[9] to peace through the ecstatic transports of Christian wisdom. The road to this peace is through

nothing else than a most ardent love of the Crucified, which so transformed Paul into Christ when he *was rapt to the third heaven* that he declared: *With Christ I am nailed to the Cross; it is now no longer I that live, but Christ lives in me.*[10] This love so absorbed the soul of Francis too that his spirit shone through his flesh the last two years of his life, when he bore the most holy marks of the Passion in his body.[11]

The figure of the six wings of the Seraph, therefore, brings to mind the six stages of illumination, which begin with creatures and lead up to God, into union with Whom no one rightly enters save through the Crucified. For *he who enters not by the door, but climbs up another way, is a thief and a robber. But if anyone enter* by this door, *he shall go in and out and shall find pastures.*[12] For this reason Saint John writes in the Apocalypse: *Blessed are they who wash their robes in the blood of the Lamb, that they may have the right to the tree of life, and that by the gates they may enter into the city*;[13] that is to say, no one can enter by contemplation into the heavenly Jerusalem unless he enters through the blood of the Lamb as through a door. For no one is in any way disposed for divine contemplations that lead to spiritual transports[14] unless, like Daniel, he is also *a man of desires.*[15] Now, such desires[16] are enkindled in us in two ways, to wit, through *the outcry of prayer*, which makes one sigh *from anguish of heart,*[17] and through *the refulgence of speculation* by which the mind most directly and intensely turns itself toward the rays of light.

4. Wherefore, it is to groans of prayer[18] through Christ Crucified, in Whose blood we are cleansed from the filth of vices,[19] that I first of all invite the reader. Otherwise he may come to think that mere reading will suffice without fervor,[20] speculation[21] without devotion, investigation without admiration, observation without exultation, industry without piety, knowledge without love, understanding without humility, study without divine grace, the mirror without divinely inspired wisdom. To those, therefore, who are already disposed by divine grace, to the humble and pious, to the contrite and devout, to those who are anointed *with the oil of gladness,*[22] to the lovers of divine wisdom and to those inflamed with a desire for it, to those who wish to give themselves to glorifying, admiring, and even savoring God,[23] to those I propose the following considerations, wishing at the same time to warn them that the mirror of the external world put before them is of little or no avail unless the mirror of our soul has been cleansed and polished. First, then, O man of God, arouse in yourself remorse of conscience before you raise your eyes to the rays of Wisdom reflected in its mirrors,

lest perchance from the very beholding of these rays you fall into a more perilous pit of darkness.

5. I have thought it well to divide this tract into seven chapters, prefixing titles for the easier understanding of the matters about which we must speak. I entreat the reader to consider the intention of the writer more than the work, the sense of the words more than the uncultivated style, the truth more than the adornment, and the exercise of the affections more than the instruction of the mind. He who would achieve this ought not to run perfunctorily through these considerations, but rather take his time and mull them over.

CHAPTER HEADINGS

HERE BEGINS THE REFLECTION OF THE POOR MAN IN THE DESERT

CHAPTER ONE

THE STEPS IN THE ASCENT TO GOD AND THE CONSIDERATION OF HIM THROUGH HIS VESTIGES IN THE UNIVERSE

1. *Blessed is the man whose help is from you; in this vale of tears he has determined in his heart to ascend by steps to the place which he has hoped for.*[24] Since happiness is nothing else than the enjoyment of the Supreme Good, and the Supreme Good is above us, no one can enjoy happiness unless he rise above himself, not, indeed, by a bodily ascent, but by an ascent of the heart. But we cannot rise above ourselves unless a superior power raise us. However much, then, the steps of our interior progress may be well-ordered, we can do nothing unless divine aid support us. This divine aid is at hand for all who seek it with a truly humble and devout heart, that is by sighing for it in this vale of tears by fervent prayer. Prayer, then, is the mother and origin of every upward striving of the soul. Thus Dionysius, in his book, *Mystical Theology*, wishing to instruct us in the transports of soul, opens first with a prayer.[25] Let us, therefore, also pray and say to the Lord, our God: *Lead me in your way, O Lord, that I may walk in your truth; let my heart rejoice that it may revere your name."*[26]

2. By so praying, we are given light to discern the steps of the soul's ascent to God. For we are so created that the material universe itself is a ladder by which we may ascend to God. And among things, some are vestiges, others, images;[27] some corporeal, others, spiritual; some temporal, others, everlasting; some things are outside us, and some within. In order to arrive at the consideration of the First Principle, which is the most spiritual being and eternal and above us, we must pass through vestiges which are corporeal and temporal and outside

5

us. This is what is meant by *being led in the way of God*. Next, we must enter into our mind, which is the image of God, an image which is everlasting,[28] spiritual, and within us. And this is *to walk in the truth of God*. Finally, looking to the First Principle, we must go beyond to what is eternal, most spiritual, and above us. This is *to rejoice in the knowledge and reverence of the Majesty of God*.

3. This triple way of seeing,[29] then, is equivalent to the three days' journey in the wilderness. It is like the threefold enlightenment of each day: the first is like evening; the second like morning; and the third like noon day. It reflects the threefold existence of things: in matter, in the understanding, and in the Eternal Art, according to which it was said: *Let it be, He made it,* and *it was made*.[30] Finally, it reflects the threefold substance in Christ, Who is our ladder: His corporeal substance, His spiritual substance, and His divine substance.

4. In keeping with this threefold progression, our mind has three principal ways of perceiving.[31] In the first way it looks at the corporeal things outside itself, and so acting, it is called animality or sensibility. In the second, it looks within itself and into itself, and is then called spirit. In the third, it looks above itself, and is then called mind. All three ways should be employed to ascend to God, so that He may be loved *with the whole heart, and with the whole soul, and with the whole mind*.[32] Herein lies the perfect observance of the Law and at the same time in this is found Christian wisdom.

5. Each of the foregoing ways of seeing may be subdivided according to whether we consider God as the *Alpha* or the *Omega*,[33] or whether we consider Him in any one of the aforesaid ways as through or as in a mirror. Or we may consider each of these ways in itself or in conjunction with another that is related to it. Therefore, these three principal steps of ascent must be increased to six in number.[34] Thus, just as God created the whole world in six days and on the seventh day rested, so man, the microcosm, is led in a most ordered way, through six progressive steps of enlightenment, to the quiet of contemplation. Symbolically, the ascent to the throne of Solomon rose by six steps;[35] the Seraphim that Isaias saw had six wings;[36] after six days the Lord *called Moses out of the midst of the cloud*;[37] and as St. Matthew tells us, it was *after six days* that Christ *led them up a high mountain by themselves, and was transfigured before them*.[38]

6. Corresponding, therefore, to the six steps in the ascent to God, there are six gradated powers of the soul,[39] whereby we ascend from the lowest things to the highest things, from things outside us to those

that are within, and from the temporal to the eternal. These six powers are the senses, imagination, reason, understanding, intelligence, and the summit of the mind or the spark of synderesis.[40] We have these powers implanted within us by nature, deformed through sin, reformed through grace. They must be cleansed by justice, trained by knowledge, and perfected by wisdom.

7. According to the original disposition of nature, man was created fit for the quiet of contemplation and thus *God placed him in the paradise of pleasure.*[41] But turning away from the true light to a changeable good, he and all his descendants were by his fault bent over[42] by original sin, which infected human nature in a twofold manner: the mind with ignorance, and the flesh with concupiscence. The result is that man, blinded and bent over, sits in darkness and does not see the light of heaven, unless grace comes to his aid—with justice to fight concupiscence, and with knowledge and wisdom to oppose ignorance. These effects are brought about through Jesus Christ, *who has become for us God-given wisdom, and justice, and sanctification, and redemption.*[43] For since He is the power and the wisdom of God, the incarnate Word is *full of grace and of truth.*[44] He has made grace and truth, for He infuses into us the grace of charity which, since it springs up *from a pure heart and a good conscience and faith unfeigned,*[45] rectifies the whole soul in the threefold way of seeing mentioned above. He has taught the knowledge of truth according to the three ways of approaching theology:[46] the symbolic, the proper, and the mystical, so that through symbolic theology we may rightly use sensible things, through proper theology, we may rightly use intelligible things, and through mystical theology, we may be rapt to ecstatic transports.

8. He, therefore, who wishes to ascend to God must first avoid sin, which deforms nature. He must bring the natural powers of the soul under the influence of grace, which reforms them, and this he does through prayer; he must submit them to the purifying influence of justice, and this, in daily acts; he must subject them to the influence of enlightening knowledge, and this, in meditation; and finally, he must hand them over to the influence of the perfecting power of wisdom, and this in contemplation.[47] For just as no one arrives at wisdom except through grace, justice, and knowledge, so it is that no one arrives at contemplation except through penetrating meditation, holy living, and devout prayer. And since grace is the foundation for righteousness of the will, and for the penetrating enlightenment of reason, we must first of all pray. Next, we must live holily. Then we must gaze at the

spectacles of truth, and by gazing at them, rise step by step until we
reach *the mountain height where the God of gods is seen on Zion.*[48]

9. Now since it is necessary to ascend Jacob's ladder[49] before we
can descend it, let us place our first step in the ascent at the bottom,
setting the whole visible world before us as a mirror through which
we may pass over to God, the Supreme Creator. Thus we shall be as
true Hebrews passing over from Egypt to the land promised to the
patriarchs;[50] we shall also be Christians passing over with Christ *from
this world to the Father;*[51] we shall be lovers of the Wisdom Who calls
to us and says: *Pass over to me all you who desire me, and be filled with
my fruits. For, from the greatness and the beauty of the creature comes a
knowledge of their Creator.*[52]

10. The supreme power, wisdom, and goodness of the Creator shine
forth in created things[53] in so far as the bodily senses inform the interior
senses. This is done in a threefold way. For the bodily senses serve
the intellect when it investigates rationally, or believes faithfully, or
contemplates intellectually. He who contemplates considers the actual
existence of things; he who believes, the habitual course of things; he
who investigates with his reason, the mighty excellence of things.

11. In the first way of seeing, the observer considers things in
themselves and sees in them weight, number, and measure:[54] weight
in respect to the place towards which things incline; number, by which
things are distinguished; and measure, by which things are determined.
Hence he sees in them their mode, species, and order, as well as
substance, power, and activity. From all these considerations the observer can rise, as from a vestige, to the knowledge of the immense
power, wisdom, and goodness of the Creator.

12. In the second way of seeing, the way of faith, the believer
considers this world in its origin, development, and end.[55] For *by faith
we understand that the world was fashioned by the Word of God;*[56] by
faith we believe that the periods of the three laws—of nature, of the
Scriptures, and of grace—followed one another and have flowed on
in a most orderly way; by faith we believe that the world must come
to an end in the final judgment. In the first of these beliefs we consider
the power of the highest Principle; in the second, His Providence; and
in the third, His Justice.

13. In the third way of seeing, he who investigates with his reason
sees that some things merely exist, that others exist and live, that still
others exist, live, and discern. He also sees that the first of these are
the lesser ones, the second are intermediate, and the third are the

better. Likewise, he sees that some things are merely corporeal, while others are partly corporeal and partly spiritual. From this observation he realizes that others are wholly spiritual, better and of more dignity than the first two modes of being. Moreover, he sees that some of these things are changeable and corruptible, such as terrestial things; others are changeable and incorruptible, such as celestial things. And from this observation he realizes that some things are changeless and incorruptible, that is, supercelestial things. Therefore, from visible things the soul rises to the consideration of the power, wisdom, and goodness of God, in so far as He is existing, living, intelligent, purely spiritual, incorruptible, and immutable.

14. We may extend this consideration to the sevenfold general properties of creatures, which bear a sevenfold witness to the power, wisdom, and goodness of God, if we consider the origin, greatness, multitude, beauty, plenitude, activity, and order of all things.[57] The origin of things, according to their creation, distinction,[58] and adornment[59] as the work of the six days, proclaims the power of God that produced all things out of nothing, the wisdom of God that clearly differentiated all things, the goodness of God that lavishly adorned all things. The greatness of things also—looking at their lengthy extension, breadth, and depth, at the immense power extending itself in all directions, as is clear in the diffusion of light, and at the efficiency of their inner, uninterrupted and diffusive operation, as is manifest in the action of fire—clearly portrays the immensity of the power, wisdom, and goodness of the Triune God, Who, uncircumscribed, exists in all things by His power, presence, and, essence.[60] Likewise, the multitude of things in their generic, specific, and individual diversity of substance, form, or figure, and the efficiency which is beyond all human estimation, manifestly suggests and shows the immensity of the three above-mentioned attributes in God. The beauty of things, too, if we but consider the diversity of lights, forms, and colors in elementary, inorganic, and organic bodies, as in heavenly bodies and in minerals, in stones and metals, and in plants and animals, clearly proclaims these three attributes of God. In so far as matter is full of forms because of the seminal principles,[61] and form is full of power because of its active potentialities, while power is capable of many effects because of its efficiency, the plenitude of things clearly proclaims the same three attributes. In like manner, manifold activity, whether natural, cultural, or moral, by its infinitely multiple variety, shows forth the immensity of that power, art,[62] and goodness, which is for all things "the cause of being, the

basis of understanding, and the norm of orderly conduct."[63] Finally, when we consider order in reference to duration, position, and influence, that is, from the standpoint of prior and posterior, superior and inferior, more noble and more ignoble, it clearly points out, first of all, in the book of creation, the primacy, sublimity, and dignity of the First Principle in regard to the infinity of His power; secondly, in the book of Scriptures, the order of divine laws, commands, and judgments shows the immensity of His wisdom; and lastly, in the body of the Church, the order of the divine Sacraments, rewards, and punishments reveals the immensity of His goodness. So it is that order itself leads us to that which is first and highest, most powerful, most wise, and best.

15. Therefore, whoever is not enlightened by such great splendor in created things is blind; whoever remains unheedful of such great outcries is deaf; whoever does not praise God in all these effects is dumb; whoever does not turn to the First Principle after so many signs is a fool. So, open your eyes, alert the ears of your spirit, unlock your lips, and apply your heart[64] that you may see, hear, praise, love, and adore, magnify, and honor your God in every creature, lest perchance the entire universe rise against you. For because of this, *the whole world shall fight against the unwise.*[65] But on the other hand, it will be a matter of glory for the wise, who can say with the prophet: *For you have given me, O Lord, a delight in your doings, and in the work of your hands I shall rejoice. How great are your works, O Lord! You have made all things in wisdom; the earth is filled with your riches.*[66]

CHAPTER TWO

THE CONSIDERATION OF GOD IN HIS VESTIGES IN THIS VISIBLE WORLD

1. We may behold God in the mirror of visible creation, not only by considering creatures as vestiges of God, but also by seeing Him in them; for He is present in them by His essence, His power, and His presence. And because this is a higher way of considering than the preceding one, it follows as the second step of contemplation, on which level we ought to be led to the contemplation of God in every creature that enters our mind through the bodily senses.

2. It should be noted that this world, which is called the *macrocosm*, enters our soul, the *microcosm*, through the portals of the five senses in so far as sense objects are apprehended, enjoyed, and judged. This may be illustrated in the following way. In the visible world there are some things that generate, others that are generated, and still others that govern them both. Those things that generate are simple bodies, such as the heavenly bodies and the four elements. For everything that is generated or produced by a natural agency must be generated and produced from these elements through the power of light[67] that harmonizes the contrariety of the elements in composite things. Those things that are generated are bodies composed of the elements, as are minerals, plants, animals, and human bodies. Those that govern both those that generate and those that are generated are spiritual substances, which may either be completely bound up with matter, as the souls of brutes, or separably linked with it, as are rational spirits; or they may be altogether free from matter, as are the celestial spirits, which the philosophers call Intelligences, and we call angels.[68] According to the philosophers, it is the function of these latter to move the heavenly bodies. Consequently, the administration of the universe is attributed to them, inasmuch as they receive from the first cause, God, an influx of power which they, in turn, dispense in the work of administration that has to do with the natural stability of things. According to the theologians, however, the ruling of the universe is attributed to the angels according to the command of the most high God with reference

to the works of reparation. Accordingly they are called *ministering spirits, sent to serve for the sake of those who shall inherit salvation.*[69]

3. Man, therefore, who is called a microcosm, has five senses that serve as five portals through which the knowledge of all things existing in the visible world enters his soul. For through sight enter sublime and luminous bodies, and all other colored things; through touch, solid and terrestrial bodies; through the three intermediate senses, intermediate bodies;[70] the moist through taste, the aerial through hearing, the vaporous through smell. These last have in them something of the humid, something of the airy, and something of the fiery or the hot, as is evidenced in the aroma from spices.

Through these portals, then, both simple bodies and composite bodies made up of simple ones enter the soul. We perceive by the senses not only particular sense objects, such as light, sound, smell, taste, and the four primary qualities[71] which the sense of touch apprehends, but also common sense objects,[72] such as number, size, form, rest, and motion. And since everything that is moved is moved by another,[73] and since, also, certain things move and come to rest of themselves—animals, for instance—we are led, when we perceive bodily motion through the five senses, to the knowledge of spiritual movers, as from an effect to the knowledge of causes.

4. The whole of this visible world, then, in its three classes of things, enters the human soul through apprehension.[74] These visible and external things are what first enter the soul through the doors of the five senses. Yet these enter, not through their substances, but through similitudes generated in the medium, and pass then from the medium into the organ. From the external organ they pass into the internal organ, and thence into the apprehensive faculty. Thus, the generation of the species in the medium, and its passing from the medium to the organ, and the turning of the apprehensive faculty upon it leads to the apprehension of all those things which the soul apprehends from outside itself.

5. From this apprehension, if it is of a suitable object, pleasure follows.[75] Properly speaking, the senses are delighted in an object, perceived through the abstracted similitude, either by reason of its beauty as in sight, or by reason of its sweetness as in smell or hearing, or by reason of its wholesomeness as in taste and touch. For all pleasure is founded on proportion. But since the species shares the character of form, power, and activity, according to the relation it has to the source from which it emanates, to the medium through which it passes,

or to the goal for which it aims, so proportion is observed in the similitude in so far as it has the character of the species or form, and then it is called beauty, because "beauty is nothing other than numbered equality, or a certain disposition of parts, together with a suavity of color."[76] Again, proportion is observed in so far as it has the character of power or strength, and then it is called sweetness, when the acting power does not disproportionally exceed the recipient sense. For the senses are pained by extremes and delighted by moderation. Finally, proportion is observed in so far as it has the character of efficacy and effect, which is proportionate when the agent, by its action, satisfies a need of the recipient. This the agent does by protecting and nourishing the recipient, and this is most apparent in taste and touch. Thus through pleasure, external delights enter the soul by means of their similitudes, according to any of the three kinds of pleasure.

6. After this apprehension and delight, there follows judgment[77] by which one not only decides whether this thing is black or white, for this pertains to a particular sense, or whether it is wholesome or harmful, for this pertains to an internal sense, but it even judges and gives an account of why this object delights. In this act of judging, one inquires into the reason for the pleasure which the senses derive from the object. Now when we inquire into the reason why an object is beautiful, sweet, and wholesome, we find that it consists in a certain proportion of equality. But the nature of equality is the same in both large and small objects: it is not increased by dimensions; neither does it change or pass away with things that change; nor is it altered by movements. It abstracts, therefore, from place and time and motion, and for this reason it is immutable; nor can it have any limits in space and time; it is absolutely spiritual. Judgment, therefore, is an action which, by purifying and abstracting the sensory likeness received sentiently by the senses, causes it to enter into the intellective faculty. And so this whole external world must enter the human soul through the doors of the senses, according to the three aforementioned activities.

7. Yet, all these activities are vestiges in which we can perceive our God. For, since the perceived species is a similitude generated in the medium and then impressed on the organ itself, and through this impression it leads us to its starting point, that is, to the object to be known, this process manifestly suggests that the Eternal Light begets from itself a Likeness, a coequal consubstantial, and coeternal Splendor. We can perceive that He Who is the *image of the invisible God* and *the brightness of his glory and the image of his substance*,[78] Who is everywhere

by His first generation like an object that generates its similitude in the entire medium, is united by the grace of union to the individual of rational nature as the species is united with the bodily organ, so that through this union He may lead us back to the Father, as to the Fountain-head and Object. If, therefore, all knowable things must generate a likeness of themselves, they manifestly proclaim that in them, as in mirrors, can be seen the eternal generation of the Word, the Image, and the Son, eternally emanating from God the Father.

8. Similarly, the species which delights because it is beautiful, sweet, and wholesome leads one to realize that there exists a first beauty, sweetness, and wholesomeness in that first Species, in which there is the utmost proportion to and equality with the One generating. In this first Species there is power, intimated, not by means of phantasms, but by the truth of apprehension. In this first Species also there is an impact that preserves, satisfies, and completely dispels the needs of the beholder. Therefore, if *delight is the union of the suitable with the suitable*,[79] and if the Likeness of God alone has the character of that which is most beautiful, most sweet, and most wholesome, and if it is united in truth, intimacy, and a plenitude that fills every capacity, it can be seen clearly that in God alone is the fountain of true delight and that from all other delights we are led on to the seeking of Him.

9. Judgment, however, leads us in a still more excellent and more immediate way to a surer beholding of eternal truth.[80] For, if judgment has to be made by reason that abstracts from place, time, and change, and hence also from dimension, succession, and mutability, it is made by a reason which is immutable and without limits in time or space. But nothing is absolutely immutable and unlimited in time and space unless it is eternal, and everything that is eternal is either God or in God. If, therefore, everything which we judge in a more certain manner, we judge by such a reason, then the following is clear: God is for all things the reason and the infallible rule and the light of truth. All things shine forth in this light in a manner which is infallible and indelible, in a manner which does not admit of doubt or possibility of refutation or second judgment on our part, or change, or limit in space and time, and in a manner that is indivisible and intellectual. Therefore, those laws by which we judge with certainty about all sense objects that come to our knowledge, since they are laws that are infallible and indubitable to the intellect of him who apprehends, since they cannot be eradicated from the memory of him who recalls, for they are always present, since they do not admit of refutation or judgment by the

intellect of him who judges, because, as St. Augustine says, "No one judges of them but by them,"[81] these laws must be changeless and incorruptible, since they are necessary. They must be without limits in space because they are not circumscribed by any place. They must be without limits in time since they are eternal, and for this reason they cannot be divided into parts since they are intellectual and incorporeal, not made but uncreated, existing eternally in the Eternal Art, by which, through which, and according to which all beautiful things are formed. Therefore they cannot be judged with certainty except by that Eternal Art which is not only the form that produces all things, but also the form that conserves and differentiates them, for this is the Being that contains the form in all creatures, and is the rule that directs the form in all things. Through it our mind judges all things that enter it through the senses.

10. This speculation is extended by considering the seven differences of numbers by which, as by seven steps, we ascend to God, as St. Augustine makes clear in his books, *On True Religion* and *On Music*, Book Six.[82] In these passages he points out the differences of numbers, which ascend step by step from these visible creatures to the Artificer of all numbered things, so that God may be seen in all of them.

He declares that there are numbers in bodies and especially in sounds and voices, and these he calls "sounding numbers." Secondly, there are numbers which are drawn from these and which are received into the sense faculty, and these he calls "reacting numbers." Thirdly, there are numbers that proceed from the soul into the body, as is clear in gesturing and in dancing, and these he calls "forthcoming numbers." Fourthly, there are numbers in the pleasures of the senses, which result when the attention turns towards the likenesses they have perceived, and these he calls "sensuous numbers." Fifthly, there are numbers retained in the memory, and these he calls "memorial numbers." Sixthly, there are numbers by which we judge all the foregoing numbers, and these he calls "judicial numbers," which, as has been said, are necessarily above the mind, since they are infallible and beyond any evaluation on our part. These last are the ones that impress on our minds the "artistic numbers," which, however, St. Augustine does not enumerate in the classification because they are linked with the "judicial numbers." And from these "artistic numbers" also flow the "forthcoming numbers" from which are created the numerous forms of artifacts. Thus from the highest numbers, through the intermediate, to the lowest, there is a gradated descent. And to the highest numbers in turn, we ascend step by step from the "sounding numbers," by means of the intermediate "reacting," "sensuous," and "memorial numbers."

Therefore, since all things are beautiful and in some way delightful, and since beauty and delight do not exist without proportion, and since proportion exists primarily in numbers, all things are subject to number. Hence "number is the principal exemplar in the mind of the Creator,"[83] and in things, the principal vestige leading to Wisdom. And since number is most evident to all and very close to God, it leads us, by its sevenfold distinction, very close to Him; it makes Him known in all bodily and visible things when we apprehend numerical things, when we delight in numerical proportions, and when we judge irrefutably by the laws of numerical proportions.

11. From these first two steps by which we are led to behold God in vestiges, like the two wings drooping about the feet of the Seraph,[84] we can gather that all creatures in this visible world lead the spirit of the contemplative and wise man to the eternal God. For creatures are shadows, echoes, and pictures of that first, most powerful, most wise, and most perfect Principle, of that first eternal Source, Light, Fullness, of that first efficient, exemplary and ordering Art. They are the vestiges, images, and displays presented to us for the contuition of God, and the divinely given signs wherein we can see God. These creatures are exemplars, or rather illustrations offered to souls as yet untrained, and immersed in the senses, so that through these sensible things that they see they may be transported to the intelligible which they do not see, as through signs to that which is signified.

12. For creatures of this visible world signify the invisible things of God:[85] partly, because God is the Origin, Exemplar, and End of every creature,—and every effect is a sign of its cause; every example a sign of its exemplar; and every way a sign of the end to which it leads,— partly by their own power of representation; partly because of their prophetic prefiguring; partly because of angelic operation; partly also by virtue of supernatural institution. For every creature is by its very nature a figure and likeness of eternal Wisdom, but especially a creature that has been raised by the Spirit of Prophecy to prefigure spiritual things in the book of Scriptures; and more especially those creatures in whose figures it pleased God to appear through the ministry of the angels; and, finally, and most especially, any creature which He chose to institute for the purpose of signifying, and which not only has the character of sign in the ordinary sense of the term, but also the character of sacrament as well.

13. From all this, one can gather that *since the creation of the world his invisible attributes are clearly seen, being understood through the things that are made.*[86] *And so they are without excuse*[87] who are unwilling to take notice of these things, or to know, bless, and love God in them, since they are unwilling to be transported *out of darkness into the marvelous light*[88] of God. *But thanks be to God through our Lord, Jesus Christ,* Who has transported us *out of darkness into his marvelous light,* since by these lights externally given, we are disposed to reenter the mirror of our mind, wherein shine forth divine things.

CHAPTER THREE

THE CONSIDERATION OF GOD THROUGH HIS IMAGE IMPRINTED ON OUR NATURAL POWERS

1. The first two steps, by leading us to God through the vestiges through which He shines forth in all creatures, have thereby led us to reenter[89] into ourselves, that is, into our mind, where the divine image shines forth. Now it is, on a third step, that entering into ourselves, and, as it were, forsaking the outer court, we ought to strive to see God through a mirror in the Sanctuary,[90] that is, in the area before the Tabernacle.[91] Here the light of Truth, as from a candelabra, will shine upon the face of our mind,[92] in which the image[93] of the most Blessed Trinity appears in splendor.

Enter into yourself, therefore, and observe that your soul loves itself most fervently. It could not love itself unless it knew itself, nor could it know itself unless it summoned itself to memory, for we do not grasp any thing with our understanding unless it is present to our memory. From these considerations notice, not with your bodily eyes, but with the eye of your mind,[94] that your soul has three powers. Consider, therefore, the activities of these three powers and their relationships, and you will be able to see God through yourself as through an image; and this indeed is to *see through a mirror in an obscure manner.*

2. The function of the memory[95] is to retain and represent not only present, corporeal, and temporal things, but also successive, simple, and everlasting things. It retains the past by remembrance, the present by receiving things into itself, and the future by foresight. It retains also simple things which are the principles of continuous and discrete quantities, such as a point, an instant, and a unit, without which it is impossible to bring to our memory or to think of things which stem from them. It retains also in a permanent way the principles and axioms[96] of the sciences. For, as long as one uses reason he can never forget them, so that on hearing them again he would approve and give his assent to them not as though he perceives them anew, but rather recognizes them as innate and familiar. That this is so becomes clear when one proposes the following principle: "Each thing is either af-

firmed or denied"; or "Every whole is greater than its part";[97] or any other axiom that may not be contradicted in the "interior discourse of the soul."

In its first activity, the actual retention of all things in time—past, present, and future—the memory is an image of eternity, whose indivisible present extends itself to all times. From its second activity, it is evident that the memory has to be informed not only from the outside by phantasms but also from above, by receiving and having in itself simple forms that cannot enter through the doors of the senses, nor through sensible phantasms. From the third activity, we hold that the memory has present in itself a changeless light in which it recalls changeless truths. And thus it is clear from the activities of the memory that the soul itself is an image of God and a similitude so present to itself and having Him so present to it that it actually grasps Him and potentially "is capable of possessing Him and of becoming a partaker in Him."[98]

3. The activity of the intellective faculty consists in understanding the meaning of terms, propositions, and inferences. The intellect grasps the meaning of terms when it understands by a definition what each thing is. But a definition must be given in more general terms; these, in turn, must be defined by others still more general, until we arrive at the highest and most general. If these last are unknown, we cannot understand the less general by way of definition. Consequently, unless one knows what being *per se* is, he cannot fully know the definition of any particular substance.[99] But being *per se* cannot be known unless it is known together with its properties, which are one, true, and good. And since being can be understood as incomplete or as complete, as imperfect or as perfect, as in potency or in act, as existing in a qualified or in an unqualified manner, as a part or as a whole, as transient or permanent, as existing through something else or *per se*, as mixed with non-being or as pure being, as dependent or as absolute, as posterior or prior, as changeable or unchangeable, as simple or composite, and since "privations and defects can in no way be known except through something positive,"[100] therefore our intellect does not make a full and ultimate analysis of any single created being unless it is aided by a knowledge of the most pure, most actual, most complete and absolute Being, which is Being unqualified and eternal, and in Whom are the essences of all things in their purity. For how could the intellect know that a specific being is defective and incomplete if it had no knowledge of the Being that is free from all defect? And in like manner may we reason about the other properties mentioned before.

Secondly, the intellect can be said truly to comprehend the meaning of propositions when it knows with certainty that they are true; and to know in this way is really to know, for it cannot be deceived in such comprehension. Since it knows that this truth cannot be otherwise, it knows also that this truth is changeless. But since our mind itself is changeable, it could not see this truth shining forth in so changeless a manner were it not for some other light absolutely and unchangeably resplendent; nor can this light possibly be a created light subject to change. The intellect, therefore, knows in that light *that enlightens every man who comes into the world*, which is the *True Light* and *the Word in the beginning with God.* [101]

Finally, our intellect only then truly grasps the meaning of an inference when it sees that the conclusion follows necessarily from the premises and when it sees this inference not only in necessary but also in contingent matters, as, for example, "If a man runs, a man moves." Our mind perceives this necessary relationship not only in regard to existent things, but also in regard to non-existent ones. For just as it follows, granted a man's existence, that "If a man runs, a man moves," so also does the same conclusion follow if he does not exist at all. But such necessity of inference does not follow from the existence of the thing in matter, since it is contingent; nor from its existence in the mind, because that thing would be merely a fiction in the mind if it did not exist in reality. Hence it must come from the exemplar of it in the Eternal Art, according to which things have a link and relation to one another that follows their representation in the Eternal Art. Thus, as St. Augustine says in *On True Religion*, [102] "The light of one who reasons truly is enkindled by that Truth and strives to go back to It." From this it is manifestly evident that our understanding is joined to eternal Truth Itself, and if this light does not teach, no truth can be grasped with certitude. You are able, then, to see within yourself the Truth that teaches you, if desires and sensory images do not hinder you and become as clouds between you and the ray of Truth.

4. The activity of the elective faculty is found in counsel, judgment, and desire. Counsel consists in inquiring which is better, this or that. But something can be said to be better only because it approaches the best. The approach to the best, however, is greater the more it is like the best. No one therefore knows whether this thing is better than that unless he knows that this is to a higher degree more like the best. And no one knows that one thing is more like another unless he knows the other. For I do not know that this man is like Peter unless I know or

recognize Peter. Therefore, a knowledge of the highest good must necessarily be impressed on all who give counsel.[103]

Moreover, a sure judgment in regard to things about which we give counsel is made according to some law. No one, however, judges with certainty according to a law unless he is certain that the law is right and that he should not be a judge of it. But our mind does judge about itself. And since the mind cannot judge the law according to which it makes judgments, that law is higher than our mind. The mind judges according to this law because it is stamped on the mind. But there is nothing higher than the human mind save only Him who made it. Therefore, in its judging, our deliberative faculty reaches the divine laws, if it makes a full and ultimate analysis.

Finally, desire[104] is concerned principally with what moves it most, but that moves it most which is loved most, and what is loved most is happiness. But happiness is not attained unless the best and ultimate end is possessed. Human desire, therefore, seeks whatever it seeks only because of the highest Good, because what it seeks either leads to the highest Good or has some likeness to it. So great is the power of the highest Good that nothing can be loved by a creature except through the desire for that Good, so that he who takes the likeness and the copy for truth errs and goes astray.

See, therefore, how close the soul is to God, and how, through their activity, memory leads us to Eternity, intelligence to Truth, and the elective faculty to the highest Good.

5. Moreover, if one considers the order, the origin, and the relationship of these faculties to one another, he is led up to the most blessed Trinity Itself. For, from memory comes forth intelligence as its offspring, because we understand only when the likeness which is in the memory emerges at the high point of our understanding and this likeness is the mental word.[105] From the memory and the intelligence is breathed forth love, as the bond of both. These three—the generating mind, the word, and love—exist in the soul as memory, intelligence, and will, which are consubstantial, coequal, equally everlasting and mutually inclusive. If God, therefore, is a perfect spirit, then He has memory, intelligence, and will. He also has a Word[106] begotten and a Love breathed forth, which are necessarily distinct, since one is produced by the other—a production, not of another essence, nor merely of an accidental difference, but a production of a distinct Person.

The mind, then, when it considers itself by looking into itself as through a mirror, rises to the speculation of the Blessed Trinity, the

Father, the Word, and Love, Three Persons coeternal, coequal and consubstantial, so that whatever is in any one is in the others, but one is not the other, but all three are one God.[107]

6. To achieve this reflection which the soul has of its unique principle that is triune through the trinity of its powers, by which it is the image of God, it is aided by the lights of the sciences which perfect and inform it, and represent the most blessed Trinity in a threefold manner. For all philosophy is either natural, or rational, or moral. The first is concerned with the cause of being, and thus leads to the Power of the Father; the second is concerned with the basis of understanding, and thus leads to the Wisdom of the Word; the third deals with the ordering of our life and thus leads to the Goodness of the Holy Spirit.[108]

Furthermore, the first, natural philosophy, is divided into metaphysics, mathematics, and physics.[109] Metaphysics deals with the essences of things; mathematics, with numbers and figures; and physics, with natures, powers, and diffusive operations. Thus the first leads to the first Principle, the Father; the second, to His Image, the Son; and the third, to the gift of the Holy Spirit.

The second, rational philosophy, is divided into grammar, which makes men capable of expressing themselves; logic, which makes them keen in argumentation; and rhetoric, which makes them apt to persuade or move others. This likewise suggests the mystery of the most Blessed Trinity.

The third, moral philosophy, is divided into individual, familial, and political. The first of these suggests the unbegotten nature of the First Principle; the second, the familial relationship of the Son; and the third, the generosity of the Holy Spirit.

7. All these branches of knowledge have certain and infallible laws as lights and beacons shining down into our mind from the eternal law. And thus our mind, enlightened and overflooded by so much brightness, unless it is blind, can be guided through looking at itself to contemplate that eternal Light. And, in truth, the consideration of this Light's irradiation raises up in admiration the wise; but on the contrary, the unwise, who do not believe so that they may understand, it leads to confusion. Hence is fulfilled the prophecy: *You enlighten wonderfully from the everlasting mountains. All the foolish of heart were troubled.*[110]

CHAPTER FOUR

THE CONSIDERATION OF GOD IN HIS IMAGE REFORMED THROUGH THE GIFTS OF GRACE

1. Since we contemplate the First Principle not only by going through us, but also within us, and since this kind of consideration is more excellent than the former, therefore it serves as the fourth step in contemplation. It seems strange indeed that after what has been shown of God's closeness to our souls there are so few concerned about perceiving the First Principle within themselves. Yet, the explanation of this is immediately at hand. Distracted by many cares, the human mind does not enter into itself through the memory; beclouded by sense images, it does not come back to itself through the intelligence; and drawn away by the concupiscences, it does not return to itself through the desire for interior sweetness and spiritual joy. Therefore, completely immersed in things of sense, the soul cannot re-enter into itself as the image of God.

2. And just as, when one has fallen, he must lie where he is unless someone join him and lend a hand to raise him up,[111] so our soul could not be perfectly lifted up out of these things of sense to see itself and the eternal Truth in itself had not Truth, taking on human form in Christ, become a ladder restoring the first ladder that had been broken in Adam.

Thus it is that, no matter how enlightened one may be by the light coming from nature and from acquired knowledge, he cannot enter into himself to delight in the Lord[112] except through the mediation of Christ, Who says, *I am the door. If anyone enter by me he shall be safe, and shall go in and out, and shall find pastures.*[113] But we do not come to this door unless we believe in Him, hope in Him, and love Him. Therefore, if we wish to enter again into the enjoyment of Truth as into Paradise, we must enter through faith, hope, and love of the Mediator between God and men, Jesus Christ, Who is like *the Tree of life in the midst of Paradise.*[114]

3. The image of our soul, therefore, must be clothed with the three theological virtues, by which the soul is purified, enlightened, and

perfected.[115] In this way the image is reformed and made conformable
to the heavenly Jerusalem, and becomes a part of the Church Militant,
which according to the Apostle, is the offspring of the heavenly Jerusalem. For he says, *That Jerusalem which is above is free, which is our
mother.*[116] The soul, therefore, now believing and hoping in Jesus Christ
and loving Him, Who is the incarnate, uncreated, and inspired Word—
the Way, the Truth, and the Life[117]—when she by faith believes in
Christ as in the uncreated Word, Who is the Word and the brightness
of the Father,[118] recovers her spiritual hearing and sight,[119]—her hearing to receive the words of Christ, and her sight to view the splendors
of that Light. When the soul longs with hope to receive the inspired
Word, she recovers, by her desire and affection, the spiritual sense of
smell. When she embraces with love the Incarnate Word, inasmuch
as she receives delight from Him and passes over to Him in ecstatic
love, she recovers her sense of taste and touch. Having recovered the
spiritual senses, the soul now sees, hears, smells, tastes, and embraces
her beloved, and can sing as the bride of the *Canticle of Canticles*, which
was composed for the exercise of contemplation proper to the fourth
step. No one reaches this except him who receives it,[120] for it consists
more in the experience of the affections than in the considerations of
the mind. It is at this step, where the interior senses have been restored
to see what is most beautiful, to hear what is most harmonious, to
smell what is most fragrant, to taste what is most sweet, and to embrace
what is most delightful, that the soul is prepared for spiritual transports
through devotion, admiration, and exultation, corresponding to the
three exclamations uttered in the *Canticle of Canticles*. The first of these
is uttered out of the abundance of devotion, by which the soul becomes
as a pillar of smoke of aromatic spices, of myrrh and frankincense. The
second is uttered out of the exuberance of admiration by which the
soul becomes as the dawn, the moon, and the sun, according to the
degree of enlightenment that lifts up the soul to admire the Bridegroom
whom she contemplates. The third is uttered out of the superabundance
of exultation, because of which the soul is made to overflow *with delights*
of most sweet pleasure, *leaning* wholly *upon her beloved.*[121]

4. When these things have been attained, our spirit is made hierarchical[122] so that it may continue upward to the degree that it is in
conformity with the heavenly Jerusalem. For into this heavenly Jerusalem no one enters unless it first comes down into his heart by grace,
as St. John beheld in the Apocalypse.[123] It comes down into our heart
when, by the reformation of the image, the theological virtues, the

delights of the spiritual senses, and uplifting transports, our spirit becomes hierarchical, that is, purified, enlightened, and perfected. Thus our spirit is sealed with the nine degrees of orders, when in its inner depths the following are arranged in proper order: announcing, dictating, guiding, ordering, strengthening, commanding, receiving, revealing, and anointing, and these correspond, step by step, to the nine orders of angels. In the human mind the first three degrees of the aforementioned orders concern nature; the following three, activity; and the last three, grace. Having obtained these, the soul, entering into itself, enters into the celestial Jerusalem, where, considering the order of the angels, it sees in them God, who dwells in them and performs all their works. That is why St. Bernard says in his letter to Pope Eugene IV[124] that "God in the Seraphim loves as charity, in the Cherubim knows as truth, in the Thrones resides as equity, in the Dominations he prevails as majesty, in the Principalities he rules as power, in the Powers he guards as salvation, in the Virtues he acts as strength, in the Archangels he reveals as light, and in the Angels he assists as kindness." From all this, God is seen to be as *all in all*[125] when we contemplate Him in our minds where He dwells through the gifts of the most bountiful love.

5. On this level of contemplation the study of the divinely revealed Sacred Scriptures is most especially helpful, as philosophy was for the preceding step. For Sacred Scripture is concerned principally with the work of reparation. Hence it treats mainly of faith, hope, and charity, by which the soul must be reformed, and most especially of charity. The Apostle says that charity is the end of the commandment, inasmuch as it stems *from a pure heart and a good conscience and faith unfeigned*. It is the *fulfillment of the Law*, the same Apostle says.[126] And our Savior asserts that the whole Law and the Prophets depend on these two commandments,[127] the love of God and of our neighbor. These two are found united in the one Spouse of the Church, Jesus Christ, Who is at one and the same time our Neighbor and our God, our Brother and our Lord, our King and our Friend, the Word incarnate and the uncreated Word, our Maker and our Re-maker, the *Alpha* and the *Omega*,[128] Who is also the supreme Hierarch, Who purifies, enlightens, and perfects His spouse, that is, the whole Church and every sanctified soul.

6. All Sacred Scripture, therefore, treats of this Hierarch and of the hierarchy of the Church.[129] By it we are taught how to be purified, enlightened, and perfected according to the threefold law handed down:

the law of nature, the law of Scriptures, and the law of grace. Or rather, they correspond to its three principal parts, the Law of Moses which purifies, the Prophetic Revelation which enlightens, and the Evangelical doctrine which perfects. Or more especially, they correspond to its three spiritual meanings: the tropological which purifies for righteousness of life, the allegorical which enlightens for clearness of understanding; and the anagogical which perfects through spiritual transports and the most sweet perceptions of wisdom. All this takes place in keeping with the three aforementioned theological virtues, the reformed spiritual senses, the three spiritual transports, and the hierarchical acts of the mind by which it turns back to its interior, there to see God *in the brightness of his saints*;[130] and there as in her resting place she sleeps in peace and rests[131] while the bridegroom beseeches that the spouse may not be awakened until she pleases to come forth.[132]

7. Thus by these two intermediate steps through which we enter into the contemplation of God within us as in mirrors of created images, like the two middle wings of the Seraph spread for flight,[133] we can understand how we are guided to things divine through the rational soul itself and its naturally implanted faculties, considered in their activities, their relationships, and their possession of sciences. This is apparent from the explanation of the third step. We are also guided by the reformed faculties of the soul itself. This takes place with the help of freely given virtues, spiritual senses, and spiritual transports. And this becomes clear in the fourth step. Moreover we are guided by the hierarchical activities of the human soul, its purification, enlightenment, and perfection, and by the hierarchical revelations of Sacred Scripture, given to us by the angels, according to the word of the Apostle that the Law was given *by angels through a mediator*.[134] And finally, we are led through the hierarchies and the hierarchical orders which must be arranged in our mind as they are in the heavenly Jerusalem.

8. Filled with all these intellectual lights, our mind like the house of God is inhabited by Divine Wisdom; it is made a daughter, a spouse, and a friend of God; it is made a member, a sister, a co-heir of Christ the Head; it is made the temple of the Holy Spirit, faith laying the foundation, hope building it up, and sanctity of soul and body dedicating it to God. All this is accomplished by the most sincere love of Christ, which *is poured forth in our hearts by the Holy Spirit who has been given to us*,[135] without Whom we cannot know the mysteries of God. For no

one can *know the things of a man save the spirit of the man which is in him. Even so, the things of God no one knows but the Spirit of God.*[136] Let us, therefore, be rooted and grounded in charity *that we may be able to comprehend with all the saints what is the length* of the eternity, the breadth of the generosity, the height of the majesty, and the depth of the discerning Wisdom of God.[137]

CHAPTER FIVE

THE CONSIDERATION OF THE DIVINE UNITY THROUGH ITS PRIMARY NAME WHICH IS *BEING*

1. It is possible to contemplate God not only outside us and within us but also above us: outside, through vestiges of Him; within, through His image; and above, through the light that shines upon our mind.[138] This is the light of Eternal Truth, since "our mind itself is immediately informed by Truth Itself."[139] Those who have become practiced in the first way of contemplation have already entered the atrium before the Tabernacle; those who have become practiced in the second have entered into the Sanctuary; and those who are practiced in the third, enter with the High Priest into the Holy of Holies, where the two Cherubim of Glory stand over the Ark, overshadowing the Mercy-Seat.[140] By these Cherubim we understand the two kinds or grades of contemplation of the invisible and eternal things of God: the first considers the essential attributes of God; the second, the proper attributes of the three Persons.

2. The first approach fixes the soul's gaze primarily and principally on Being Itself, declaring that the first name of God is *He Who is*.[141] The second approach fixes the soul's gaze on the Good Itself, saying that this is the first name of God. The former looks especially to the Old Testament, which proclaims chiefly the unity of the divine essence. Hence it was said to Moses, *I am Who am*.[142] The latter looks to the New Testament, which determines the plurality of the Divine Persons by baptizing *in the name of the Father, and of the Son, and of the Holy Spirit*.[143] Thus it is that Christ, our Master, wishing to raise up to the perfection of the Gospel the youth who had observed the Law, attributed to God principally and exclusively the name of *Goodness*. For He says, *No one is good but only God*.[144] Hence St. John Damascene, following Moses, says that *He who is* is the first name of God; whereas Dionysius, following Christ, says that *Good* is the first name of God.[145]

3. He, therefore, who wishes to contemplate the invisible things of God in relation to the unity of His essence should fix the attention of his soul on Being Itself and see that Being Itself is so absolutely certain

that it cannot be thought not to be,[146] because the most pure Being Itself does not come to our mind except with the full flight of non-being, in the same way as absolute nothing does not come to our mind except with the full flight of being. Just as, therefore, complete nothingness contains nothing of being or of its attributes, so contrariwise, being itself contains nothing of non-being, either in act or in potency, in objective truth or in our estimate of it. But since non-being is the privation of being, it does not come into the intellect except by means of being. Being, however, does not come to us by means of something else, because everything that is grasped by the intellect is grasped either as non-being, or as being in potency, or as being in act. If, therefore, non-being cannot be grasped except through being, and if being in potency cannot be understood except through being in actuality, and if being designates the pure actuality of being, then being is that which first comes into the intellect, and this being is that which is pure act. But this being is not a particular being which is a limited being, since any such particular being is mixed with potentiality. Neither is it analogous being, for that has the least actuality, since it least exists. It remains, therefore, that the being which we are considering is the Divine Being.[147]

4. Strange, then, is the blindness of the intellect which does not consider that which it sees before all others and without which it can recognize nothing.[148] But just as the eye, intent on the various differences of color, does not see the light through which it sees other things, or if it does see, does not notice it, so our mind's eye, intent on particular and universal beings, does not notice that Being which is beyond all categories, even though it comes first to the mind, and through it, all other things. Wherefore it appears most true that "as the eye of the bat is disposed towards the light, so the eye of our mind is disposed towards the most evident things of nature."[149] Thus our mind, accustomed as it is to the opaqueness in beings and the phantasms of visible things, seems to itself to be seeing nothing when it gazes upon the light of the highest being. It does not understand that this very darkness is the supreme illumination of our mind,[150] just as when the eye sees pure light, it seems to be seeing nothing.

5. Behold, if you can, this most pure Being,[151] and you will find that it cannot be thought of as a being attained through something else. Hence, it must necessarily be thought of as absolutely first, and it cannot come into existence from nothing or from something else. For what else exists of itself if Being itself is not due to itself and not

dependent on something else? This most pure Being, likewise, appears to you as absolutely lacking in non-being, and therefore as having no beginning and no end, but as eternal. Furthermore, it appears to you as having nothing whatsoever except this very being itself, and, hence, as having no composition, but as most simple. It appears to you as having nothing of possibility, since every possible being has in some way something of non-being, and hence it is supremely and in the highest degree actual. It appears to you as having no defect and thus is most perfect. Finally, it appears to you as having no diversity,[152] and because of this, is supremely one.

Therefore, that Being which is pure being and simple being and absolute being is the primary being, the eternal, the most simple, the most actual, the most perfect and supremely one.

6. And these things are so certain that their opposites cannot be thought of by one who really understands being itself; and one of these characteristics of Being necessarily implies the other. For since it is unqualifiedly being, therefore it is unqualifiedly first; and since it is unqualifiedly first, therefore it has not been made by another, nor could it be made by itself; hence it is eternal. Again, since it is the first and eternal, it is, therefore, not composed of other things, and hence is most simple. And because it is first, eternal, and most simple, it has nothing of possibility in it that is mixed with act, and thus it is most actual.[153] Again, because it is first, eternal, most simple, and most actual, it is most perfect; for such a Being lacks absolutely nothing, nor can any addition be made to it. And since it is first, eternal, most simple, most actual, and most perfect, therefore it is supremely one. For what is asserted by a superabundance of every kind is asserted unqualifiedly to possess all perfection. But "that which is asserted by superabundance in an unqualified manner can apply to one thing alone."[154] Hence, if "God" is the name of the being that is first, eternal, most simple, most actual, and most perfect, such a being cannot be thought not to be, nor can it be thought to be other than one. *Hear, therefore, O Israel, the Lord our God is One Lord.*[155]

If you realize this in the pure simplicity of your mind, you will be enlightened to some extent by the illumination of Eternal Light.

7. Furthermore, you have here something to lift you up in admiration. For being itself is both the first and last; it is eternal and yet most present; it is most simple and yet the greatest; it is most actual and still most changeless; it is most perfect and nonetheless immense; it is supremely one and yet pervades all things. Admiring all these

considerations with a pure mind,[156] you will be flooded with a still greater light when you behold further that pure being is precisely the last because it is the first. For since it is first, it does all things for itself, and thus the first being is of necessity the ultimate end; it is the beginning and the fulfillment, the *Alpha* and the *Omega*.[157] Thus, it is entirely present precisely because it is eternal. For, as it is eternal, it does not proceed from another, nor does it lack anything on its part, nor does it progress from one state into another; and therefore it has neither past nor future being, but only a present being. And it is greatest because it is most simple. For since it is utterly simple in essence, it is greatest in power, because the more a power is concentrated in one, the more it is infinite. Further, it is most changeless because it is most actual. As most actual, it is, therefore, pure act; and that which is pure actuality can acquire nothing new, nor lose anything that it already has; hence it cannot be changed. Likewise, because it is most perfect, it is immense. As it is most perfect, one can think of nothing better, nobler, of higher dignity beyond it, and consequently, of nothing greater, and every such being is immense. Finally, it pervades all things, because it is supremely one. For that which is supremely one is the all-embracing principle of all diversity. Hence this being is the universal, efficient, exemplary, and final cause of all things, since it is the "cause of being, the basis of understanding, and the norm for the orderly way of living." Therefore, pure being is all-pervasive, not as if it were the essence of all things, but as the supremely excellent and most universal and sufficient cause of all essences. And its power is supremely infinite and pervasive in its efficiency because it is supremely one in its essence.

8. Once more retracing our steps, let us say that because the most pure and absolute being which is unqualifiedly being is the first and the last, it is therefore the origin and the fulfilling end of all things. As eternal and most present, it encompasses and enters all durations, existing, as it were, at one and the same time as their center and their circumference. Likewise, because it is the most simple and the greatest, it is wholly within all things and wholly outside them; hence it is "the intelligible sphere, whose center is everywhere and whose circumference is nowhere."[158] As most actual and changeless, it is that which, "remaining unmoved itself, gives movement to all things."[159] Further, because it is most perfect and immense, it is within all things without being contained by them; it is outside all things without being excluded by them; it is above all things without being aloof; it is below all things without being dependent on them. Finally, since it is supremely one

and yet pervasive, it is *all in all*,[160] even though all things are many and it is itself but one. And this is so because through its supremely simple unity, its most serene truth, and its most sincere goodness, it contains in itself all power, all exemplarity, and all communicability. Hence *from him and through him and unto him are all things*,[161] for He is all-powerful, all-knowing, and all-good. To behold Him perfectly is a most blessed thing, as it was said to Moses: *Therefore I will show to you all good things.*[162]

CHAPTER SIX

THE CONSIDERATION OF THE MOST BLESSED TRINITY IN ITS NAME WHICH IS *THE GOOD*

1. Having considered the essential attributes of God, we must raise the eyes of our intelligence to the contuition of the most Blessed Trinity, so as to place the second Cherub facing the first.[163] Now just as Being itself is the principal source of the vision of the essential attributes of God, as well as the name through which the others become known, so the Good itself is the principal foundation of the contemplation of the personal emanations.[164]

2. Behold, therefore, and observe that the highest good is unqualifiedly that than which no greater can be thought. And this good is such that it cannot rightly be thought of as non-existing, since to exist is absolutely better than not to exist. And this good exists in such a way that it cannot rightly be thought of unless it is thought of as triune and one. For good is said to be self-diffusive, and therefore the highest good is most self-diffusive.[165] But this highest diffusion cannot be unless it be actual and intrinsic, substantial and hypostatic, natural and voluntary, free and necessary, unfailing and perfect. Unless there were in the highest good from all eternity an active and consubstantial production, and a hypostasis of equal nobility, as is the case with one who produces by way of generation and spiration, —thus there belongs to the first Principle from all eternity a co-producer—so that there is the loved and the beloved, the generated and the spirated, that is, the Father, and the Son, and the Holy Spirit, that is to say, unless these were present, there would not be found the highest good here, because it would not be supremely self-diffusive. For the diffusion that occurred in time, in the creation of the world, is no more than a focal point or brief moment in comparison with the immense sweep of the eternal goodness. From this consideration of creation one is led to think of another and a greater diffusion—that in which the diffusing good communicates to another His whole substance and nature. Nor would He be the highest good were He able to be wanting in this, whether in reality or even in thought.

If, therefore, you are able to behold with the eye of your mind the purity of that goodness which is the pure act of the Principle that loves with a love both free and due and a mixture of both, a love which is the fullest diffusion by way of nature and will, and also a diffusion by way of the Word in which all things are expressed, and by way of the Gift, in which all other gifts are given,—if you can do this, then you can see that through the utmost communicability of the Good, there must exist a Trinity of the Father, the Son, and the Holy Spirit.[166] By reason of Their supreme goodness,[167] the three Persons must necessarily have supreme communicability; by reason of their supreme communicability they must necessarily have supreme consubstantiality; and by reason of their supreme consubstantiality, they must have supreme likeness in their nature. Then, by reason of all these, they must have supreme coequality, and hence supreme coeternity. Finally, from all the foregoing taken together, they must have supreme mutual intimacy, by which one Person is necessarily in the other by reason of their supreme identity, and one acts with the other because of the absolute indivision of the substance, power, and activity of the Most Blessed Trinity Itself.

3. But when you contemplate these things, take care that you do not think you can understand the incomprehensible. For you have still something else to consider in these six characteristics, which forcibly strike the eye of our mind with awesome admiration. For here we have supreme communicability side by side with a character proper to each Person, and supreme consubstantiality side by side with a plurality of hypostases, and supreme identity of nature side by side with distinct Personality, and supreme coequality side by side with order, and supreme coeternity side by side with emanation, and supreme mutual intimacy side by side with the emanantion of Persons. Who would not be lifted up in admiration at the sight of such great wonders? But we know with absolute certainty that all these things are in the most blessed Trinity, if we but raise our eyes to the all-excelling Goodness. If, therefore, there is supreme communication and true diffusion, then there is also true origin and true distinction. And, since the whole is communicated and not a part merely, then whatever is had is given, and given completely. As a result, He who proceeds and He who produces are distinguished by their properties and yet are one and the same in essence. Since, then, they are distinguished by their properties, it follows that they have personal properties and plurality of hypostases, and an emanation of origin, and an order, not of time but of origin.

And the emanation does not consist in local motion but in freely given inspiration by reason of the authority which the Producer, as Sender, has over the One Sent. Moreover, since they are really one in substance, they must possess oneness of essence, of form, of dignity, of eternity, of existence, and of infinity. And while you consider these things, one by one, you have the subject matter that will enable you to contemplate Truth. When you compare them with one another, you have the subject matter that lifts you to the utmost heights of admiration. Therefore, that your mind may rise, through admiration, to admiring contemplation, you must consider all these attributes together.

4. For the Cherubim who faced each other symbolize a comparative approach. For, mystery is not lacking in the fact that they faced each other, *their faces being turned toward the Mercy-Seat,*[168] that thus might be verified what Our Lord says in the Gospel of St. John: *Now this is eternal life, that they may know You the only true God, and him whom You have sent, Jesus Christ.*[169] For we must admire the characteristics of the divine essence and of the divine Persons, not only in themselves, but also in comparison with the most marvelous union of God and man in the unity of the Person of Christ.

5. If you are one of the Cherubim contemplating the essential attributes of God, and if you are amazed at the fact that the divine Being is both first and last, eternal and most present, most simple and without limit, wholly everywhere and nowhere contained, most actual and never moved, most perfect and without any superfluity or deficiency, and yet immense and boundlessly infinite, supremely one and yet supremely pervasive, containing in Himself all things—all power, all truth, all goodness—if, then, you are this Cherub, gaze at the Mercy-Seat and be amazed. For in that Mercy-Seat the first Principle is joined with the last. God is joined with man, who was formed on the sixth day;[170] the eternal is joined with time-bound man, in the fullness of time born of the Virgin; the most simple is joined with the most composite; the most actual is joined with Him Who suffered supremely and died; the most perfect and immense is joined with that which is small; He who is both supremely one and supremely pervasive is joined to an individual that is composite and distinct from others, that is to say, the man Jesus Christ.

6. And if you are the other Cherub and contemplate that which is proper to the Persons, and if you are amazed that communicability coexists with personal identity, consubstantiality with plurality, a unity of nature with personality, coequality with order, coeternity with pro-

duction, and mutual intimacy with emanation—for the Son is sent by the Father, and the Holy Spirit by both the Father and the Son, and yet the Holy Spirit sent from both ever remains with them and never departs from them. If you are this Cherub, now face toward the Mercy-Seat and be amazed that in Christ a personal unity coexists with a trinity of substances and with a duality of natures. In Christ also a perfect accord coexists with a plurality of wills, a mutual predication of God and man coexists with a plurality of proper attributes; a co-adoration coexists with a multiplicity of honors; and a coexaltation over all things coexists with a diversity of dignities; and finally that codominion coexists with a plurality of powers.

7. In this contemplation consists the perfect illumination of our mind, when, as it were, on the sixth day it sees man made to the image of God. For, if an image is an expressed likeness, then when our mind contemplates in Christ the Son of God, Who is by nature the image of the invisible God,[171] our humanity so wonderfully exalted, so ineffably united, and when at the same time it sees united the first and the last, the highest and the lowest, the circumference and the center, the *Alpha* and the *Omega*, the caused and the cause, the Creator and the creature, that is, *the book written within and without*, it has already reached something that is perfect. Thus it arrives at the perfection of its illuminations on the sixth step, as God did on the sixth day. And now nothing further remains but the day of rest on which through transports of mind the penetrating power of the human mind *rests from all the work that it has done.*

CHAPTER SEVEN

THE SPIRITUAL AND MYSTICAL TRANSPORT OF THE MIND IN WHICH REST IS GIVEN TO OUR UNDERSTANDING AND OUR AFFECTION PASSES OVER ENTIRELY TO GOD

1. Accordingly, the mind has reached the end of the way of the six contemplations. They have been like the six steps by which one arrives at the throne of the true Solomon and at peace, where, as in an inner Jerusalem, the true man of peace rests with a tranquil soul. These six reflections are also like the six wings of the Cherubim, by which the mind of the true contemplative, flooded by the light of heavenly wisdom,[172] is enabled to soar on high. They are also like the first six days during which the mind must be at work so that it may finally reach the Sabbath of rest.

After our mind has beheld God outside itself through and in vestiges of Him, and within itself through and in an image of Him, and above itself through the similitude of the divine Light shining above us and in the divine Light itself in so far as it is possible in our state as wayfarer and by the effort of our own mind, and when at last the mind has reached the sixth step, where it can behold in the first and highest Principle and in the Mediator of God and men, Jesus Christ,[173] things the like of which cannot possibly be found among creatures, and which transcend all acuteness of the human intellect—when the mind has done all this, it must still, in beholding these things, transcend and pass over, not only this visible world, but even itself. In this passing over, Christ is the way and the door;[174] Christ is the ladder and the vehicle, being, as it were, the Mercy-Seat above the Ark of God and *the mystery which has been hidden from eternity*.[175]

2. He who turns his full countenance toward this Mercy-Seat and with faith, hope, and love, devotion, admiration, joy, appreciation,

praise and rejoicing, beholds Christ hanging on the Cross, such a one celebrates the Pasch, that is, the Passover, with Him. Thus, using the rod of the Cross, he may pass over the Red Sea,[176] going from Egypt into the desert, where it is given to him to taste the *hidden manna;*[177] he may rest with Christ in the tomb, as one dead to the outer world, but experiencing, nevertheless, as far as is possible in this present state as wayfarer, what was said on the Cross to the thief who was hanging there with Christ: *This day you shall be with me in Paradise.*[178]

3. This also was shown to the Blessed Francis, when, in a transport of contemplation on the mountain height—where I pondered over the matter that is here written—there appeared to him the six-winged Seraph fastened to a cross, as I and many others have heard from the companion who was then with him at that very place. Here he passed over into God in a transport of contemplation. He is set forth as an example of perfect contemplation, just as previously he had been of action, like a second Jacob-Israel.[179] And thus, through him, more by example than by word, God would invite all truly spiritual men to this passing over and this transport of soul.

4. In this passing over, if it is to be perfect, all intellectual activities ought to be relinquished[180] and the loftiest affection transported to God, and transformed into Him. This, however, is mystical and most secret, *which no one knows except him who receives it,*[181] and no one receives it except him who desires it, and no one desires it except he who is penetrated to the marrow by the fire of the Holy Spirit, Whom Christ sent into the world.[182] That is why the Apostle[183] says that this mystical wisdom is revealed by the Holy Spirit.[184]

5. And since, therefore, nature avails nothing and human endeavor but little, little should be attributed to inquiry, but much to unction; little to the tongue, but very much to interior joy; little to the spoken or written word, but everything to the Gift of God, that is, to the Holy Spirit. Little or nothing should be attributed to the creature, but everything to the Creative Essence—the Father, the Son, and the Holy Spirit. And thus, with Dionysius,[185] we address the Triune God: "O Trinity, Essence above all essence, and Deity above all deity, supremely best Guardian of the divine wisdom of Christians, direct us to the supremely unknown, superluminous, and most sublime height of mystical knowledge. There new mysteries—absolute and changeless mysteries—of theology—are shrouded in the superluminous darkness of a silence that teaches secretly in a most dark manner that is above all manifestation and resplendent above all splendor,[186] and in which

everything shines forth—a darkness which fills invisible intellects by an abundance above all plenitude with the splendors of invisible good things that are above all good." All this pertains to God.

To the friend, however, for whom these words were written, we can say with Dionysius: And you, my friend, in this matter of mystical visions, renew your journey, "abandon the senses, intellectual activities, and all visible and invisible things—everything that is not and everything that is—and, oblivious of yourself, let yourself be brought back, in so far as it is possible, to union with Him Who is above all essence and all knowledge. And transcending yourself and all things, ascend to the superessential gleam of the divine darkness by an incommensurable and absolute transport of a pure mind."

6. If you wish to know how these things may come about, ask grace, not learning; desire, not understanding; the groaning of prayer, not diligence in reading; the Bridegroom, not the teacher; God, not man; darkness, not clarity; not light, but the fire that wholly inflames and carries one into God through transporting unctions and consuming affections. God Himself is this fire, and *His furnace is in Jerusalem;*[187] and it is Christ who enkindles it in the white flame of His most burning Passion. This fire he alone truly perceives who says: *My soul chooses hanging, and my bones, death.*[188] He who loves this death can see God, for it is absolutely true that *Man shall not see me and live.*[189]

Let us, then, die and enter into this darkness. Let us silence all our cares, our desires, and our imaginings. With Christ crucified, let us pass *out of this world to the Father,* so that, when the Father is shown to us, we may say with Philip: *It is enough for us.* Let us hear with Paul: *My grace is sufficient for you,*[190] and rejoice with David, saying: *My flesh and my heart have fainted away: You are the God of my heart, and the God that is my portion forever. Blessed be the Lord forever, and let all the people say: so be it, so be it. Amen.*[191]

NOTES TO THE TEXT

Prologue

1 *In the beginning . . . the very first Beginning.* The "first beginning" is, of course, God, the source of all things. In order to bring out the many Christian associations of this declaration, the Latin sentence "In principio primum principium" has been translated literally. Most likely Saint Bonaventure wanted his opening words to carry associations with the opening words of Genesis (1, 1), "In the beginning God created heaven and earth . . ." and with the opening words of the Gospel of Saint John (1,1), "In the beginning was the Word. . . ." In his *Sermons on the Six Days of Creation (Collationes in Hexaëmeron,* 1, 10; V, 331), he writes: "It is clear that one must begin from the place where the two outstanding men of wisdom began, namely Moses and John, the first and last voices of the wisdom of God. The former said: 'In the beginning God created heaven and earth,' . . . and John said: 'In the beginning was the Word, and the Word was with God, and the Word was God.'" We must begin our study of creation from the perspective of divine wisdom, since the creature cannot be understood rightly without that approach. Only through the divine revelation in the sacred Scriptures do we discover the deeper roots of our nature and all finite things—that we owe our existence to the creative goodness of God. Only then do we begin to understand our being rightly. To begin with the first beginning, or God, and to come down to the truth of created realities, then, is characteristic of the method of Saint Bonaventure. It could aptly be called 'a theology from above,' but 'theology from above' must be understood here from Saint Bonaventure's perspective.

2 *from . . . the Father of Lights.* This text of The Epistle of Saint James (1, 17) expresses one of the central ideas in Bonaventurean philosophy and theology. It occurs in many of his works. He opens *The Reduction of the Arts to Theology (De reductione artium ad theologiam;* V, 319) with this text of Saint James and then explains: "These words of sacred Scripture not only indicate the source of all illumination; they likewise point out the generous flow of the manifold rays which issue from that Fount of light." And he declares in the opening pages of *The Breviloquium (Breviloquium;* V, 201) that: "The Scriptures have their origin not in human research but in a divine revelation coming from the Father of Lights." "The Father of Lights" is, even more than 'The Good' of Plato, the beginning of all things. He is the source of the existence, the light, and the goodness of all created things.

3 James 1, 17.

4 Ephesians 1, 17; Luke 1, 79; Philippians 4, 7; John 14, 27.

5 *peace.* The word 'peace' has many layers of meaning in the patristic and medieval Christian tradition. 'Peace,' in a first sense of the term, meant for Roman Christians of the early years of the Christian era not so much the end of war, as it did for other Romans, but rather the cessation of persecution.

Yet, it had another deeper Christian sense, and this was the peace which Christ brought to his followers, the peace between man and God which Christ the mediator achieved through his redemptive death. Believers in Christ were 'children of peace' and Christ himself as the achiever of peace was called 'Peace.' 'Peace' further implied belief in the Christ who achieved the 'peace' between God and men. Such belief was confirmed in baptism, and this confirmation brought peace and enrolled its recipients in the community of the Church. In their worship the members of this Church gave one another a 'kiss of peace' as a sign of their fraternity of belief and renewed life in Christ.

Saint Augustine, in Book XIX of *The City of God* (cc. 11–14), presents a more technical view of peace. Similar to the Platonic-Stoic definition of 'peace,' 'peace' for Augustine is "the tranquillity of *order*." Yet, Augustine challenged the *pagan order*, where the Stoic sage was at the top of the hierarchy. For the Christian believer, God is the high point of the order of reality, and until all things are reordered to God, the true apex of the order of reality, there can never be the tranquillity of the true order, with God at the top ('peace' as the Christian conceives of it).

In general, for Saint Bonaventure as for Saint Augustine, 'peace' means the tranquillity that comes from right order, where God is at the top of the hierarchy of beings. In the present context 'peace' has the meaning of the soul's rest in God, the key to right order. Saint Bonaventure himself indicates this vision of reality when he speaks of 'ecstatic peace' as the ultimate goal of the *Itinerarium*.

6 Thomas of Celano, in the first *Life of Saint Francis* (1, 10), describes the way that Saint Francis greeted people in these words: "In all his preaching, before he proposed the word of God to those gathered about, he first prayed that peace be given to them, saying: 'The Lord give you peace.' He always most devoutly announced peace to men and women, to all he met and overtook. For this reason many who had hated peace, and had hated also the salvation granted by Christ, embraced peace with all their heart. They did so through the cooperation of the Lord; and they were made children of peace and seekers after eternal salvation." Cf. also Saint Bonaventure's *Major Life of Saint Francis* III, 2 (*Legenda maior*; VIII, 510): "In all his sermons he began by wishing his hearers peace, saying to them: 'God give you peace,' a form of greeting which he had learned by a revelation, as he afterwards asserted. He was moved by the spirit of the prophets and he proclaimed peace and salvation. By his salutary warnings he united in the bond of true peace great numbers of people who had been at enmity with Christ and far from salvation."

It should be noted that the Latin title of the *Major Life of Saint Francis* is *Legenda maior*. As Fr. Damien Vorreux indicates in his explanations of Fr. Benen Fahy's translation of the *Major Life*, '*Legenda*' here, as for the entire Middle Ages, is not the antithesis of history. It is an historical account having a twofold characteristic: (1) it is meant to be read publicly, as is evident from the etymology of the word *legenda* (meaning 'it should be read publicly'), and

(2) it is controlled by and subject to the laws of literary composition, in contradistinction to the *florilegia* which are content to group anecdotes together. The *Fioretti* would be a typical example of a *florilegium*.

7 Psalm 119, 7; Psalm 121, 6; Psalm 75, 3.

8 Since Saint Francis died on October 4, 1226, the *Itinerarium* was written, or at least conceived, on Mount Alverno (thirty miles east of Florence, above the sources of the River Arno) in September or October of 1259.

9 *pass over (transitus)*. Saint Bonaventure uses this word in its many connotations. *Pascha* or passover in Egypt, the passing of the Hebrews through the Red Sea, the death of Christ (which allowed us to pass over from our sinful state to a state of reunion with God), the death of St. Francis. All these meanings are contained as layers in the broader signification of the mystical death and the mystical passing over into God that takes place through contemplative union of the mind with God. See I, 9.

10 II Corinthians 12, 2; Galatians 2, 20.

11 The stigmatization, or imprinting of the wounds of the crucified Christ in Saint Francis's body, is not only the inspiration of the *Itinerarium*, but also the model of the mystical union portrayed in the work. This is expressly stated in the *Itinerarium* VII, 3: "He [Saint Francis] is set forth as an example of perfect contemplation, just as previously he had been of action, like a second Jacob-Israel. And thus, through him, more by example than by word, God would invite all truly spiritual men to this passing over and this transport of soul."

According to Saint Bonaventure, mystical union is a union with Christ on the cross. For this reason, the stigmatization typifies the mysticism of Saint Francis and his followers. A later alternative model and approach to mysticism, based on the fifteen 'Step' Psalms (Psalms 120–134) and embued with Renaissance humanist theology, may be found in *The Journey of the Mind to God* by the Jesuit Cardinal Saint Robert Bellarmine.

12 John 10, 1 and 9.

13 Apocalypse 22, 14.

14 *spiritual transports*. This is simply another term for mystical union.

15 Daniel 9, 23.

16 *desires*. *Desire* likewise is a multilayered word. In the present context Saint Bonaventure associates it with Daniel, who is called "a man of desires." But he could also link it to Saint Augustine, who began his journey to God with the words: "You have made us for Yourself, Lord, and our heart is restless until it rests in You." Desire has a twofold source in Saint Bonaventure. Through prayer it is enkindled by the fire of the Holy Spirit, a fire that penetrates the very marrow of a man of desires. Desire is also encouraged by the exercise of reflection that Saint Bonaventure is about to undertake—where he sees how all created things in different ways lead the mind to God. Created things are thus invitations to God, invitations that we must desire to accept. The importance of desire is stressed by Saint Bonaventure in his *Sermons on*

the Six Days of Creation, XXII, 29 (V, 442): "The soul is not contemplative without a lively desire. He who lacks this hunger has no contemplative life." Saint Bonaventure encouraged his students to seek contemplative knowledge when he commented on *The Sentences of Peter Lombard*, II, d. 33, q. 2, a. 3 (*Commentarium in II Sententiarum*; II, 546): "I judge that this way of knowing should be sought by every just man in the present life." Saint Bonaventure realized that some may not be able to enjoy the contemplative knowing toward which he urges his aspiring theologians. To the simple brethren he explains in *Sermon I on Holy Saturday* (*Sabbato sancto. Sermo 1*; IX, 269): "You who are unlettered should not at the present time lose hope when you have heard these things, because the untrained cannot have such a knowledge of divine realities. Yet, you will be able to have this knowledge in the life to come." For those who can attain a contemplative knowledge of God in this life, however, desire is an essential element in its pursuit. As Saint Bonaventure tells us in his *Commentary on the Gospel of Luke*, 9, 33, n. 60 (*Commentarium in Evangelium Sancti Lucae*; VII, 235): "After the beginning of contemplation, progress in it follows. This requires two things: great joy in regard to the gift that has been given, and a strong desire to continue in the pursuit of it. . . ."

17 Psalm 37, 9.

18 *prayer.* Saint Bonaventure presents a concise and admirable theology of prayer in his paraphrase of the 'Our Father' in the *Breviloquium*, V, 10 (V, 263): "Concerning the petitions of 'The Lord's Prayer,' this is what must be held: that although God is most generous—readier to give than we are to receive—still He wills our prayers so that He might have the occasion to bestow upon us the Holy Spirit's gifts of grace. He wills us to pray not only by mental prayer, which is 'an ascent of the mind to God,' but also by oral prayer, which is 'a request for suitable things from God.' [Cf. John of Damascus, *On the Orthodox Faith*, III, 24, 248 (PG 94, 1089–90; tr. Frederic H. Chase, Jr.; New York: Fathers of the Church, Inc., 1958, 328.] He wants not only prayer coming directly from ourselves, but also prayer through the saints as through His divinely appointed assistants, so that we might obtain through their intercession what we are not worthy to merit on our own. And that we would not wander about uncertain, not knowing what we should request, God gave us a structured form of prayer, in which, under seven requests, are found all of the things that we should seek."

19 Cf. Hebrews 1, 3.

20 Cf. John 2, 20 and 27.

21 *speculation.* All the activities described in the six steps of the *Itinerarium* are speculations. In this sense, speculation is an intellectual activity of the higher reason beholding in various created objects their relation to God, their Creator. It is a kind of contemplation which links the mind to divine realities. In the human authors of the divine Scriptures this was realized through revelation: the prophetic authors were so united with the divine realities that even though they had no direct vision of them, still they could not deny their

truth. Moving on to his immediate audience, Saint Bonaventure notes in the *Breviloquium*, V, 6 (V, 260): "In just men," this contemplation of divine Truth is attained "through speculation which begins with the senses, moves on to the imagination, passes from the imagination to reason, and from reason to understanding, and from understanding to intelligence, and from intelligence to wisdom, that ecstatic knowledge which begins in this life and reaches fulfillment in everlasting glory." (Cf. also *Itinerarium*, I, 6.) In the *Itinerarium*, 'speculation,' 'contemplation,' and 'consideration' are practically synonymous. Thus, speculation is not merely any intellectual activity. It is a contemplative activity, or the intellectual activity of a contemplative soul, and only as such is it a means of enkindling desire for union with God.

'Speculation' can also have the purely intellectual, nonreligious meaning of Aristotle's *theoria*, that is, speculative science as opposed to practical science. In this sense it is equivalent to the Latin *curiositas* (vain curiosity). In the *Sermons on the Six Days of Creation*, I, 8 (V, 330), Saint Bonaventure tells us that "the curious man lacks devotion. There are many such persons, devoid of praise and devotion, though they may have all the splendors of knowledge. They make wasps' nests that have no honeycombs, whereas the bees make honey."

The contrast between the various kinds of knowledge in the writings of Saint Bonaventure is anticipated and well described by Odo Rigaud, one of Bonaventure's teachers at the University of Paris. In his *Question Concerning the Science of Theology*, Odo distinguishes four forms of knowledge (ed. L. Sileo, 19): "Furthermore, one should note here the following distinction: there is science that is science, such as the science of the liberal arts; and there is wisdom that is science, such as that of first philosophy or metaphysics, where there is no true flavor; and there is science that is wisdom, as in the Old Testament; and there is wisdom that is wisdom, as in the New Testament."

One should note that for Saint Bonaventure the Latin word '*sapientia*' (wisdom) has many meanings, but along with the aspect of knowledge that is associated with it, there is also an affective element of relish or enjoyment. When this affective element is stressed, Saint Bonaventure finds the root of the Latin word '*sapientia*' in *sapor*, meaning 'taste.' 'Wisdom' thus is knowledge of those things that we come more and more to love and relish. This is what Saint Bonaventure means by contemplative knowledge.

Saint Bonaventure lists nine opposing characteristics that contrast the purely theoretical life and the contemplative life. The harmonizing of these contrasting qualities is necessary if the teaching of the *Itinerarium* is to be followed successfully. It is difficult to attempt to assign definite meanings to the various terms. A few suggestions, however, may be helpful.

Reading. This may mean inspirational or spiritual reading, but also the public reading of lectures by a theologian. In this sense—likely the meaning intended here—'reading' would describe the teaching of theology without relish or love for God or for the world as God's creation. In his *Sermons on the Six Days of*

Creation, XXII, 21 (V, 440), Saint Bonaventure says: "Blessed Francis said that he wanted his brothers to study, but on the condition that they practiced what they taught. What good is it to know a lot and to relish nothing?"

Fervor. In his *Commentary on the Gospel of Luke,* 12, 20 (VII, 316), Saint Bonaventure quotes Saint Bernard of Clairvaux: "Reading is good, but fervor is better, since it teaches us about all things." Saint Bonaventure explains: "Fervor teaches everything since it teaches us to love God and love our neighbor."

Speculation. Here apparently it is taken in the sense of a purely theoretical activity or way of life.

Devotion. This is closely connected with unction. It implies, however, a more active attitude—a surrender in love.

Investigation. This is research in the sense of 'a delving into the depths of a question.'

Admiration. This is a sense of wonder before the deep mystery of the objects we are examining. See n. 23.

Observation. This is the form of research that pertains to breadth of learning.

Exultation. This is a sense of wonder before the manifold manifestations of God's presence in creation.

Industry. Here 'industry' is used in the sense of the untiring activity of the natural faculties. Saint Bonaventure notes many other layers of meaning connected with this word in his *Sermons on the Six Days of Creation,* XXII, 24–28 (V, 413–14): Industry must be employed to distinguish between things that are to be rejected and things that are to be chosen, and between things that are fitting and those that are unfitting, and between things that are permitted and those that are not. Industry, with the help of grace, must also be employed to do what needs to be done and to do it for God's sake. And at another level, industry likewise needs to be employed to raise the soul to divine concerns instead of purely human ones.

Piety. This is nothing else but the proper feeling, affection, and service toward the true, primary, and highest source of all things (*Sermons on the Seven Gifts of the Holy Spirit,* III, 5; *Collationes de septem donis Spiritus Sancti;* V, 469).

Knowledge. Here 'knowledge' is used in the sense of scientific knowledge. Its opposition to charity is borrowed from Saint Paul's First Letter to the Corinthians 8, 1: "Knowledge puffs one up, but charity builds." Saint Bonaventure concludes from this passage (*Sermons on the Gifts of the Holy Spirit,* IV, 24; V, 478): "Therefore, it is necessary to join charity to knowledge."

Understanding. This is insight into the richer meaning of the mysteries of God and the created world.

Study. This embraces all human endeavor, including the preceding activities. They must all be complemented by divine grace.

Mirror. All creation is a mirror. As Saint Bonaventure says in his *Sermons on the Six Days of Creation,* II, 27 (V, 340): "And so it is clear that the whole world is as a single mirror filled with illuminations reflecting the divine wisdom and shedding light like live coals." Yet, the mirror of creation is of no avail unless it be illumined by the wisdom of divine revelation. Viewed from the perspective of pure philosophy, creatures hide their deeper secrets, telling us nothing of their dependence on God for their being and truth or showing nothing of how God is present in them. Without the wisdom of divine revelation creatures fail to reflect the God who created them. They dim and hide their reflective or 'mirror' quality.

22 Psalm 44, 8.

23 *glorifying, admiring, . . . savoring God.* These are progressive stages for Saint Bonaventure. Even in the first stage of the journey, seeing that visible creation in its origin, greatness, multitude, beauty, plentitude, activity, and order bears witness to the power, wisdom, and goodness of God, we begin to glorify or praise God. In 1, 15, Saint Bonaventure tells us: "Therefore, whoever is not enlightened by such great splendor in created things is blind; whoever remains unheedful of such great outcries is deaf; whoever does not praise God in all these effects is dumb. . . ."

Admiring. Coming at later stages of the journey, admiration brings us to an ecstatic level, where the mind is overwhelmed by that "beauty, so ancient and so new" that Saint Augustine realized he came too late to love. (Cf. *Confessions*, X, 27.) Saint Bonaventure in his short work, *To Sisters: on the Perfection of Life*, V, 8 (*De perfectione vitae ad sorores*; VIII, 119), quotes Richard of St. Victor's *The Mystical Ark* (*Benjamin Maior*), V, 5 when he wants to describe such 'admiration.' "By the force of admiration, the mind is carried above itself when, illumined by divine light and held in admiration before the supreme beauty, it is shaken with such overwhelming wonder that it is completely driven out of its usual state. Like flashing lightning, the more deeply the mind is cast down in despising itself in comparison to that invisible beauty, the more sublimely and more quickly is it elevated to sublime things, stimulated by the ardor of the highest kind of desires and carried beyond itself."

Savoring. As we indicated in note 21, wisdom (*sapientia*) is a form of knowledge that is linked with affection for and relish in the object known. In his *Sermon I on Holy Saturday* (IX, 269) Saint Bonaventure quotes Exodus 24, 11: "They beheld God, and they ate and drank." In the higher levels of contemplation God fills the hunger and thirst of their souls.

Chapter One

24 Psalm 83, 6–7.

25 Pseudo-Dionysius, *Mystical Theology*, 1, 1, opens with the prayer: "O Trinity, Essence above all essence, and Deity above all deity, supremely best Guardian of the divine wisdom of Christians, direct us to the supremely unknown, superluminous, and most sublime height of mystical knowledge. There new mysteries—absolute and changeless mysteries of theology—are shrouded in the superluminous darkness of a silence that teaches secretly in

a most dark manner that is above all manifestation and resplendent above all splendor." Cf. *Itinerarium*, 7, 5.

26 Psalm 85, 11. Taking a hint from the *Itinerarium*, 1, 2, Etienne Gilson, in an essay on the technique of the medieval sermon contained in *Les idées et les lettres*, Paris, J. Vrin, 1932), 153 suggests that this text, manifesting the spirit and procedure of a sermon theme, provides an outline of the three main stages of the spiritual climb up to God in the *Itinerarium*.

"Lead me in your way" indicates our passing among the vestiges, the corporeal and temporal objects outside of us, that are examined in Chapters One and Two.

"Walk in your truth" points to the images, the spiritual and everlasting objects that are within us, that are studied in Chapter Three.

"Rejoice that it may revere your name" directs us to the similitudes, souls that have recovered their supernatural likeness to God by putting on the theological virtues and regaining their spiritual senses. These similitudes are encountered in Chapter Four.

27 For an introduction to the manner in which the created universe reflects, represents, and describes its Creator, see Etienne Gilson, *The Philosophy of Saint Bonaventure*, tr. Dom Illtyd Trethowan and Frank J. Sheed (Paterson, N.J.: St. Anthony's Guild Press, 1965), c. 7: "Universal Analogy," 185–214. For a full treatment of this question in Saint Bonaventure, see his *Commentary on Book I of the Sentences*, d. 3 (I, 66–94) and *Commentary on Book II of the Sentences*, d. 16 (II, 393–408). Saint Bonaventure offers a summary of his teaching in *The Breviloquium*, II, 12 (V, 230): "From what we have just said one can gather that creation is, as it were, a book in which its Creator, the Trinity, is reflected, represented and described according to a threefold level of expression: as a vestige, as an image, and as a likeness. The justification for creation being a vestige of the Trinity is found in all creatures; the justification for creation being an image of the Trinity is found only in intellectual or rational spiritual beings; the justification for creation being a similitude of the Trinity is found only in those who [by grace] are Godlike. From these bases, by climbing, as it were, certain steps of a ladder, the human mind is capable of ascending gradually to the highest principle, who is God."

Every creature is a vestige of the Trinity by the fact that its creation expresses in a remote but distinct manner God's power, wisdom, and goodness, attributes that are appropriated to the Father (power), Son (wisdom), and Holy Spirit (goodness). Every spiritual creature—angels and rational souls—is an image of the Trinity and therefore shows a close and distinct likeness to the three Persons of the Trinity. Every spiritual creature who is sanctified by grace is a similitude of God because it is made Godlike through the Triune God's indwelling presence and hence resembles God most closely. As we have indicated in the preceding note, Saint Bonaventure deals with the vestiges of God in Chapters One and Two of the *Itinerarium*, with the images of God in Chapter Three, and with the similitudes of God in Chapter Four.

28 *everlasting (aeviternum)*. This is not an easy word to translate. For Saint Bonaventure God alone is eternal. There are no created beings that are eternal; an eternal world or an eternal creature is impossible. Saint Bonaventure accepts everlastingness (*aevum*) as the measure of duration proper to spiritual substances, such as angels, in contrast to eternity that is proper to God alone. He also maintains that, although there might be a dispute among philosophers and theologians about the character of everlastingness, namely, whether or not it is marked by succession, the more likely and intelligible position is that everlastingness (*aevum*) is characterized by succession of existence. Cf. *Commentary on Book II of the Sentences*, d. 2, p. 1, a. 1, q. 3 (II, 62).

29 These three levels of invitation to union with God (vestiges, images, and similitudes) in the *Itinerarium* are related by Saint Bonaventure to many other threefold divisions that tie in with the theme of the work. 'Divisions into three' characterize the three-day journey of Moses into the wilderness (Exodus 3, 18), the natural distinction of the day into three periods of light (twilight, morning, noon), the threefold existence of created things (first in the mind of the divine Artist, then in the spiritual intellects, and, thirdly, in the matter in which creatures actually exist), and, lastly, the threefold union that takes place when Christ's divine nature is united with his human soul and body. Each suggests the theme of the *Itinerarium*: Moses' *journey*, the different *illuminations*, the way *creatures tell us about God*, and the focus on *Christ* who is *our ladder to God*.

30 Cf. Genesis, 1, 3. Following the interpretation given to this verse by Saint Augustine in his *Literal Commentary on 'Genesis,'* II, c. 8, nn. 16–20 (PL 34, 269–70), Saint Bonaventure explains: "They were first produced from all eternity in the divine Art, then in the intellectual creature, and thirdly in the sensible world." The Scriptural words "Let it be" refer to the expression of the ideas in God, the eternal Art. "He made it" refers to the infusion or illumination of these ideas into the angelic intellects. "It was made" refers to the creation of the visible world according to the divine ideas. On the similarities and differences between angelic and human knowledge, and for an explanation of the infusion of ideas into the angelic intellects, see Etienne Gilson, *The Philosophy of Saint Bonaventure*, c. 8: "The Angels," 215–44.

31 Three principal ways of perceiving. One approach to our way of knowing is to focus on the objects considered. Saint Bonaventure's description of our *principal* ways of perceiving follows the three different levels of objects (vestiges, images, similitudes) to which our mind will attend. When the mind considers corporeal things outside it, then it has the name 'animality' or 'sensibility.' When the same mind focuses on its own level and looks at itself, then it is called 'spirit.' When it raises its attention to things above its level, then it is called 'mind' in a more special sense of this word.

Saint Bonaventure from different perspectives divides the mind in many different ways and often uses different terms to express these operations. In the preceding paragraph we saw two different uses of the word 'mind.' Etienne Gilson, *The Philosophy of Saint Bonaventure*, c. 12: "The Illumination of the Intellect," 343–46, provides a guide to help us keep the terminology straight.

32 Mark 12, 30; cf. Matthew 22, 37 and Luke 10, 27.

33 Cf. Apocalypse 1, 8.

34 The three *principal* ways of perceiving in I, 4 (and also mentioned in n. 31) are soon (I, 6) going to be expanded into six ways of perceiving. Before he even announces these six increased ways of perceiving, Saint Bonaventure associates them with other 'sixes' that are linked to his theme of the soul's journey to God. Since his road to God will be the study of creation with its different signposts leading to their Creator, it is natural that he would see the parallel to the six days of creation, and then to the day of rest that would correspond to the soul's peace or rest in God at the end of the journey. The six steps leading up to the throne of the King of Kings reminded him of the six steps to the throne of King Solomon. Remembering the stigmata of Saint Francis, Saint Bonaventure could not forget the six-winged seraphim described by Isaiah as he saw the Lord sitting on a throne. Nor could he not remember Moses' six days in the clouds on Mount Sinai before the Lord called out to him on the seventh day, or that Christ six days after Peter confessed his belief in Him was transfigured before him and James and John, and finally revealed His divinity.

35 I Kings 10, 19.

36 Isaiah 6, 2.

37 Exodus 24, 16.

38 Matthew 16, 13–17, 8.

39 Saint Bonaventure, in his *Sermons on the Six Days of Creation*, V, 24 (V, 358), indicates the various objects of the three principal and six increased ways of perceiving with these words: "The animal power is twofold: either it looks at the objects of the particular senses or the common sense, or it attends to the phantasms of sensible things; and so we have the senses and imagination. The intellectual power is also twofold: it either considers the universal reasons of things as it abstracts them from place and time and dimension, or it is elevated to consider separated substances, and thus there are the two powers of reason and understanding—through reason it compares, through understanding it grasps itself and spiritual substances. The divine operation or power is likewise twofold: it either turns itself to grasp divine manifestations, or it turns to the enjoyment of divine favors. The first occurs through intelligence, the second through a unitive or loving power."

40 *synderesis*. This is the apex or highest power of the soul. Apparently the term goes back to Saint Jerome's *Commentary on Ezechiel*, 1, 7 (PL 25, 22; CCSL 75, 12), where he translates the Greek word used in Ezechiel 1, 7 as "spark of conscience" (*scintilla conscientiae*). Saint Bonaventure, in his *Commentary on Book II of the Sentences*, d. 39, a. 2, q. 1 (II, 908–11), portrays it as the

highest power of reason and describes it as the natural gravity of the soul toward the good. He also there distinguishes it from conscience. See also the end of n. 39 where it is given another name: the unitive or loving power.

41 Genesis 2, 15.

42 *bent over.* This image seems originally derived from Plato's *Laws* where Plato tells us that when men were bent over with fatigue the gods gave them the Muses, and Apollo their leader, and Dionysus, as companions in their feasts, so that nourishing themselves in festive companionship with the gods, they should again stand upright and erect. In its Christian form, Saint Bonaventure seems to take it from Saint Bernard's *Commentary on the Canticle of Canticles*, 80, 2 (PL 183, 1166) where Bernard refers to the Gospel of Luke 13, 10, where the crippled woman is described as "bent over and . . . quite unable to stand up straight." Saint Bonaventure deals with the theme more extensively in the introduction to his *Commentary on Book II of the Sentences* (II, 3ff.). The curvature caused by sin directs man to himself and the result is self-love and concupiscence. It must be healed by grace and a just life without selfishness. Ignorance, another effect of sin, makes man blind and prevents him from seeing the light of heaven above him. This is healed by science and wisdom.

43 I Corinthians 1, 24 and 30.

44 John 1, 14 and 17.

45 I Timothy 1, 5.

46 This division of theology should not be confused with the different senses of sacred Scripture (literal, allegorical, moral, and anagogical) that Saint Bonaventure describes in the prologue of *The Breviloquium*, 4 (V, 205) and in his *Sermons on the Six Days of Creation*, XIII, 11 (V, 389). In the very next paragraph of the latter work (XIII, 12; V, 389–90) he well describes symbolic theology which teaches how we might rightly use sensible things. Before the fall into sin man had a knowledge of sensible things and through them he was carried up to God, to praise, worship, and love him. After he fell man lost this kind of knowledge. He no longer could read the book of the world. The book of the sacred Scriptures tells us again the divine meaning of sensible things and is able to restore the symbolic character of the world, so that it once again leads us to the knowledge, praise, and love of God. This is the message of Chapters One and Two of the *Itinerarium*.

Proper theology is that which is presented in his *Commentary on the Book of the Sentences* or in *The Breviloquium*, where the theologian examines that which he believes and attempts more and more to discover its intelligibility. In the second question of the prologue of his *Commentary on Book I of the Sentences* he puts the proper theological task as a study "of the credible as made intelligible" (I, 11, n. 4). In relation to the *Itinerarium*, Chapters Three through Six provide a reflection that is properly theological.

Mystical theology deals with union with God. As Dionysius the Areopagite advises, in his *Mystical Theology* 1, 1: "Abandon the senses, intellectual activities, and all visible and invisible things—everything that is not and everything that is—and, oblivious of yourself, let yourself be brought back, in so far as it is possible, to union with Him Who is above all essence and all knowledge." These words are quoted by Saint Bonaventure in 7, 5 and are a key to Chapter Seven of the *Itinerarium*.

47 Saint Bonaventure gives greater detail concerning prayer, meditation, and contemplation in *The Triple Way* (VIII, 3–27). The titles for each chapter of this work give strong clues to the function of each of these exercises: I. On meditation, by means of which the soul is cleansed, enlightened, and perfected; II. On prayer, by means of which our misery is deplored, God's mercy is beseeched, and worship to Him is offered; III. On contemplation, by means of which true wisdom is attained. The justice that purifies or cleanses is treated under the first part of his treatment of meditation.

48 Psalm 83, 8.

49 Cf. Genesis 28, 12.

50 Cf. Genesis 12, 2–3 and 28, 13–15.

51 John 13, 1.

52 Wisdom 11, 21.

53 Saint Bonaventure borrows from Saint Augustine, especially from his *On the Trinity*, a great number of the ternaries or groups of three that he employs to illustrate how creatures manifest the wisdom, power, and goodness of God to one who develops a contemplative attitude of mind.

54 The first manifestation of the wisdom, power, and goodness of God that a contemplative mind can grasp is based on Wisdom 11, 20: "You have arranged all things by measure and number and weight." Weight is the tendency of things to seek their natural place (gravity is thought of as an inborn natural appetite of things to seek their natural place or goal). When all things are rightly placed, there is order, that is, the order of all things tending toward their final cause, God. Number defines a thing, that is, it sets borders or limits it in dimension and in perfection, making it more or less noble, and pointing to the most noble or perfect being, God. Measure is the more global or metaphysical limitation of a creature, which, in relation to God, is essentially finite and contingent, since it is an effect of God.

55 Saint Bonaventure follows Saint Augustine (*Letter 138*, 5; PL 33, 527, and *The City of God*, XII, 4; PL 41, 351–52) in his conception of history as a most beautiful drama, composed by God and acted out by mankind. The beauty of this drama and its meaning, however, can be grasped only through faith and on the basis of revelation. Since we are in such a position that we can witness only a small part of this drama, we need Holy Scripture to raise us to a point from which we can view and comprehend it in its entirety—from the creation of the world to judgment day. See the prologue of *The Breviloquium*, (V, 204): "And thus the whole universe, from beginning to end, is described by Scripture as running in a most orderly way, ordered like a wonderfully crafted drama, where one may see, as time passes by, the diversity, multiplicity, equity, order, rightness, and beauty of the many divine decrees that proceed

from God's wisdom that rules the universe. Since, however, no one can perceive the beauty of the drama unless his vision grasps it as a whole, so no one perceives the beauty of this order and regimen of the universe unless he grasps it completely. Because, however, no man lives so long as to grasp the whole with his own two eyes, and neither is he able to foresee future events on his own, the Holy Spirit has provided us with the book of the sacred Scriptures, whose length corresponds to the duration of God's rule of the universe."

For a detailed treatment of history according to Saint Bonaventure, see Joseph Ratzinger, *The Theology of History in St. Bonaventure*; tr. Zachary Hayes (Chicago: Franciscan Herald Press, 1971).

56 Hebrews 11, 3.

57 The consideration of these seven conditions of creatures is based on Hugh of Saint Victor, *Didascalicon*, VII, 1–12 (PL 176, 811–22).

58 *distinction*. Here it refers to the actual coming forth of physical nature through distinction or separation. In *The Breviloquium*, II, 2 (V, 220), Saint Bonaventure explains that this division is threefold and extends over the first three days of creation, where light was separated from darkness (first day), the waters beneath the firmament were separated from the waters above the firmament (second day), and the waters were separated from the land (third day).

59 *adornment*. This refers to the following three days of creation: luminous nature, adorned by the sun, the moon, and the stars (fourth day); perspicuous nature, water and air, adorned by the fishes and the birds (fifth day); opaque nature, land, adorned by beasts, reptiles, and man (sixth day). Cf. *The Breviloquium*, II, 2 (V, 220).

60 That God exists in all things through His power, His presence, and His essence is a time-honored formula that Saint Bonaventure explains in the following way in the *Commentary on Book I of the Sentences*, d. 37, a. 1, q. 3 (I, 648): "With these three terms Blessed Gregory describes the perfection of God's ways of existing in all the things in which He does exist, and his explanation is as follows: [1] something is in another according to the lack of distance that is characteristic of presence, the way a content is in a container, as in the case of water in a bowl; [2] something is in another according to the influence of its power, as a mover in a body that it may move; and [3] something exists in another according to a condition of intimacy, the way that something contains something within itself, as a soul in a body. And anything that exists perfectly in something has to be present in this threefold way, and this is the way that God is present in all things."

61 Seminal principles. This expression goes back to the Stoics, whose phrase for these principles was the Greek *logoi spermatikoi* (translated as 'seminal principles' or 'seminal reasons'). Saint Augustine adopted and adapted the concept and passed it on to medieval Christian thinkers like Saint Bonaventure. For Christians, God created the world out of nothing. But He does not create things out of nothing continually. He has inserted and concealed in the nursery

of this world the active and positive potentialities for new things to develop out of already existing things. A rough image would be that of a rosebud that becomes a rose. A more technical explanation of how new forms of things appear and the role that nondivine agents play in their coming forth is treated admirably by Etienne Gilson in *The Philosophy of St. Bonaventure*, c. 10: "The Animals," 265–83.

62 *art.* The word 'art' in the medieval world has a broader meaning than in today's world. For medievals it means everything that is made by man acting as a rational being. Artificial things (meaning 'things made according to art') are all the products made by man according to a rational plan. 'Art' is applied to what we today would call artistic works and also to all other things done by human ingenuity. In no way does 'artificial' mean for Saint Bonaventure what we might call 'fake' or 'not real.' When medievals say art is 'everything made by man acting as a rational being' they mean 'everything made by man in a way that brings their products toward their true goals and fulfillment.' This is achieved more fully the closer the product comes to the 'Eternal Art' or divine examplar. See below, III, 9 and III, n. 102.

63 Augustine, *The City of God*, VIII, 4 (PL 41, 228–29).

64 Cf. Proverbs 22, 17.

65 Wisdom 5, 21.

66 Psalm 91, 5 and 103, 24.

Chapter Two

67 For Saint Bonaventure the basic elements are fire, air, water, and earth. These are incompatibles, and so there must be a fifth essence or element that is common to them and is able to reconcile them. For Saint Bonaventure this quintessential element is light.

For a more detailed explanation of how light is the first substantial form of bodies and how it brings about the various compositions of the elements into inorganic and organic bodies, see Etienne Gilson, *The Philosophy of St. Bonaventure*, c. 9: "Inanimate Bodies. Light," 245–64.

68 The theory that angels have the function of governing the heavenly bodies is adopted by Saint Bonaventure as probable. Cf. *Commentary on Book II of the Sentences*, d. 14, p. 1, a. 3, q. 2 (II, 349): "God moves the heavens through a created intelligence or angel, and this follows the order that God established for the universe, and about which Augustine in his *Literal Commentary on Genesis* says: 'And God thus set up the order of the world—that he would place a spirit in authority over every body.' And so, as it is fitting that He assign angels to administer to men, so is it proper that they be assigned to the movement and routine of the heavens, since in doing this work they would also be ministering to men here on earth and serving God's majesty."

69 Hebrews 1, 14.

70 *intermediate senses, intermediate bodies.* Saint Bonaventure has in mind

here the position of the sense organs and bodies. In the human body the eyes have the highest position, and the hands, the chief organs of touch, have the lowest. Of the elements, fire reaches farthest upward, above air, and earth has the lowest position, below water.

71 *four primary qualities.* They are the hot, the cold, the moist, and the dry and are perceived by touch, which is considered the most basic sense. These qualities are called primary because they are the basic qualities of the four elements.

72 *common sense objects.* They are common because they are perceived by more than one sense, in contrast to the particular sense objects, which are perceived by one sense only.

73 Aristotle, *Physics*, VII, c. 1, t. 1 (241b 24–25).

74 *apprehension.* This is the process by which a sense grasps or apprehends an object. Since the sense object itself does not come into our eye or ear or any other sense, and yet we apprehend it, some explanation is necessary. To account for our sense knowledge we thus have to distinguish a number of different elements that play some part in our apprehension of a sense object. First, there has to be a sense object which we grasp. Since the substance of the sense object does not enter into our sense, then there must be a likeness or similitude of it that comes to us. To do so, this likeness, technically called a species, must pass from the sense object and through a medium, such as air for the eye or ear, to the sense organ. When this species or likeness comes to the external sense organ, such as the eye or ear, and then to the internal sense power or faculty, such as sight or hearing, the sense object by means of this sense likeness is perceived or apprehended. For a more detailed description of the various elements in this process of apprehension, see Etienne Gilson, *The Philosophy of St. Bonaventure*, c. 12: "The Illumination of the Intellect," 309–28.

75 Anyone who has been stunned by a surprising clap of thunder realizes that not all sense perceptions or apprehensions are pleasurable. For something to be pleasurable a certain proportion must be present between the species or likeness of the object perceived and the perceiving power or faculty. All pleasure is founded on proportion, whether the pleasure be that derived from beauty (or proportion in sight), from sweetness (or proportion in smell or hearing), or from refreshment and satisfaction (or proportion in taste or touch).

76 Augustine, *On Music*, VI, 13, 38 (PL 32, 1184); cf. *The City of God*, XXII, c. 19, 2 (PL 41, 781). This definition of beauty, as expressed in both these works of Augustine, stresses the harmonious arrangement of the parts of a picture ('a certain disposition of parts'). The other part of the definition means simply 'a harmony of color or a pleasing arrangement of colors.' In any case, proportion, or harmony, is the basis of every true pleasure.

77 *judgment.* For Saint Bonaventure, perhaps based on the parallel to the principle suggested in n. 68 that, according to the divine order of things, the higher is put in charge of the lower, something higher is always fertilizing, as

it were, that which is lower. (We will see the application of this principle in another concrete instance in discussing Saint Bonaventure's doctrine of illumination in n. 80.) In the present instance, we are able to see in the concrete sense apprehension something that transcends it, its universal, and therefore its timeless content. And of this universal and timeless measure or ground of judgment we are able both to be aware and to begin to form an idea. The function of judgment, then, is to purify the concrete sensible species of all its contingent imperfections and to conceive it in its ideal form.

78 Colossians 1, 15 and Hebrews 1, 3.

79 This definition of pleasure goes back to Avicenna (980–1037), the Moslem interpreter of Aristotle. In his commentary on Aristotle's *Metaphysics*, tr. 8, c. 7 (ed. S. Van Riet, *Avicenna latinus: Liber de philosophia prima*, V–X, p. 432, lines 67–70), Avicenna defines pleasure (*delectatio*) in this way: "Pleasure is nothing but the grasping of something agreeable at its level of agreement. Wherefore, sensible pleasure is a sensing of what is agreeable and intelligible pleasure is an understanding of what is agreeable."

80 Here we meet for the first time in this work Saint Augustine's theory of illumination. It is a doctrine frequently evoked by Saint Bonaventure, but it is a doctrine that is so central to the thought of both men, that even when they do not mention it explicitly, it still is present and influencing everything they say.

It is an undeniable fact that we make judgments about things. We say that 'this is not fair or just,' or 'that is stupid.' But on what basis do we do so? Do we ourselves decide or determine that this must be so? Is it actually we who decide or determine that this thing is or is not just, or beautiful, or harmonious? Saint Bonaventure, following Saint Augustine, says that our determination is not the reason. According to his theory, the act of judging consists in applying a standard to things that we apprehend. We measure them by a standard; we submit them to a standard that transcends them and us. Things in time and place are mutable. That by which we judge, the reason or ground for our judgments, is something unchangeable, and not just a measure for a particular place or time. But to be timeless, spaceless, and immutable are qualifications that apply to God alone. Hence, by judging how the sense objects measure up, we compare them to absolute standards or measures that shine forth in this divine light, and we thus acknowledge that they do or do not measure up.

Neither Saint Augustine nor Saint Bonaventure claims that we are conscious of this light (Cf. 5, 4). It is only later, as we reflect on the possibility of true judgment, that we realize that a measure must be present for us to do so. An analogy, or example, that might help us to understand what is going on is the following Christian version of Plato's cave: Imagine yourself in a cathedral on a sunny day, looking at the beautiful stained-glass windows there. You would see the glorious blue colors of the windows, the detailed figures of those portrayed in them, and, like many other viewers, you would be praising their beauty. Yet, imagine that you happened to visit on another day, a dark, dreary day, on which the colors did not stand out, and the figures were hardly recognizable. Even though you were in the cathedral each time, and the windows were the same, still there would be a noticeable difference. If you tried to figure out why there was such a difference, you would eventually come to realize that the sun was brightly present on the first day and was somewhat blocked out on the second day. In neither case would you have seen the sun directly. But, in trying to explain the difference in your perceptions and judgments of the beautiful windows and the figures portayed in them, you would come to realize that the light, although not visible directly, was the most important and determinant factor. In effect, such a light is the cause of our being able to see and to judge the objects that are perceived only under its indirectly perceivable presence.

This example should help us understand Saint Bonaventure's view of our judgments about sense objects. According to his theory, when we judge sense objects, we see them against a certain kind of light by which we compare them with the absolute, eternal, and necessary standards shining forth in this light. We do not see the light, but by means of it we measure the sense objects we do see. Hence it is because of this light that the ideal and necessary aspects of things that in themselves are contingent in space and time are grasped. Now, these ideal "reasons" by which we measure and judge contingent things shine forth beyond any doubt as infallibly true, and they give absolute certitude to our judgments. They are so present to us that they cannot be effaced from our memory or consciousness, since as soon as we apprehend their contingent copies (the sensible things), the ideal "reasons" shed their light over them. And since they transcend us and are the measure of our judgment, they themselves cannot be refuted, or judged, or measured. Purely spiritual, eternal, and necessary as they are, they must be in God, in the Eternal Art. As we have indicated, we do not behold these ideals or "reasons" or rules directly. It is the light of God, the Eternal Art, that illumines us and that regulates and stimulates us to grasp in the concrete the absolute and necessary content of the relative and contingent things we see. Hence, without the light from above, nothing absolute and necessary could be known; without the concrete sense objects, however, nothing would be apprehended at all. The apprehension and judgment of contingent sense objects, then, is the result of the interaction of the eternal light with the light of our reason and the contingent sense objects themselves. See also below, n. 95.

81 Augustine, *On Free Will*, II, 14 (PL 32, 260): "No one judges it, and without it no one judges rightly. Therefore, beyond a doubt it is clear that wisdom is superior to our minds, for only by it are our minds made wise, and also made to be judges, not of it, but by means of it of every other thing."

82 Saint Bonaventure here distinguishes seven different kinds of numbers, and to a great extent he follows Saint Augustine. In his *On Music*, Book VI (PL 32, 1081–1194), Augustine treats of the various kinds of rhythms. He ends Chapter 6 (PL 32, 1081–1194) by naming and ordering the various kinds

of numbers according to a hierarchy of excellence: "Let the first in order be named 'judicial' (*numeri iudiciales*), the second 'forthcoming' (*progressores*), the third 'reacting' (*occursores*), the fourth 'memorial' (*recordabiles*), and the fifth 'sounding' (*sonantes*)."

In the order of Saint Bonaventure's treatment: 1) 'Sounding' rhythms or numbers are those that exist in things that produce sound. In other words, they exist outside the soul or outside our perception of them. They are found in the bodies or in the air that give off rhythms, as in the constantly dripping drops of water that wear away a rock or in the chirps of a bird. 2) 'Reacting' numbers are rhythms as reacted to by our senses. They are the dripping or the chirps as heard or registered by our sense of hearing. 3) 'Forthcoming numbers' are the sounds that we produce, as in the rhythmic taps we make on a tambourine or the repetitious movements we perform in a dance. 4) 'Sensuous numbers' are the rhythms that bring us pleasure as they react on our senses and do so in a proportioned way, being not too loud or too soft, not too quick or too slow. 5) 'Memorial numbers' are those that stay in our memories. They last longer than the sounds themselves or our impressions and appreciations of such sounds. We can bring them back again and again. 6) 'Judicial numbers' are the undying numbers that exist in the Eternal Art. They are the ultimate source and judge of all the order, harmony, measure, and proportion of things. 7) 'Artificial numbers' are the presence of the judicial numbers in our human souls. They permit us to judge the order, harmony, measure, and proportion of all things, and they guide us in producing all our works in a more harmonious, measured, and proportioned way.

Saint Bonaventure often uses here the examples of sounds and rhythms he has taken from Saint Augustine's *De musica*, but the same theory can be applied to all things where harmony, measure, proportion, and order are involved.

The purpose of all this intricate analysis of numbers is to lead us to the realization that each level of harmony, proportion, and order in these different types of numbers permits us to climb to the ultimate source of all order and beauty found in the Eternal Art. See above, n. 62.

83 Boethius, *De arithmetica*, I, 2 (PL 63, 1083): "Everything that has been made from the first days of things seems to be formed according to numbers. For number was the principal examplar in the mind of the Creator."

84 Isaiah 6, 2.

85 Saint Bonaventure declares that every creature is a visible sign of God Who is invisible. He distinguishes four kinds of signs. The first kind is a vestige or footprint of God in creation. It is a natural manifestation of the wisdom, power, and goodness of God and is found in every creature, since every one of them shows in its makeup God's wisdom, power, and goodness.

The second kind is not a natural form of signification, but a form that depends upon divine revelation in the sacred Scriptures. This second kind is Scripture's use of certain things in the Old Testament to signify things that will be in the New Testament. For instance, the sacrificial lamb of the Old

Testament will, in the New Testament, prefigure the sacrifice of Jesus, Who is referred to as the Lamb of God. The third type of signification is also derived from the Scriptures and concerns the visible forms that God assumes by association with a creature, as in the case of the Holy Spirit taking on the form of a dove at the baptism of Christ by John the Baptist (*Matthew* 3, 16). The fourth kind of sign is that found in the Christian sacraments, where a creature, such as water, not only is used as a sign of cleansing in baptism, but also brings about a spiritual cleansing of man's sin.

86 Romans 1, 20.

87 *Ibid.*

88 I Corinthians 15, 57 and I Peter 2, 9.

Chapter Three

89 *reenter.* Saint Bonaventure, following Saint Augustine and Richard of St. Victor, and also citing a work attributed to Saint Bernard, indicates that when we go out of the Tabernacle of our minds through sense cognition, it is necessary to reenter into ourselves. In *To Sisters: on the Perfection of Life*, c. 1 (VIII, 108–9, he explains the difficulty of reentering one's self: "The human mind, distracted by worldly cares, fails to enter into itself through memory; clouded by imagination, it fails to turn toward itself through intelligence; attracted by concupiscence, it fails to return to itself through desire for inner sweetness and spiritual joy. Therefore, totally immersed in the senses, it is unable to reenter into itself as into the likeness of God. Thus, the mind, wholly wretched, knows nothing about itself." The kernel of this last sentence is taken from Saint Augustine's *Divine Providence and the Problem of Evil* (*De ordine*), c. 1, n. 3 (PL 32, 979). In the same chapter, Saint Bonaventure also quotes a work attributed to Saint Bernard: "Return to yourself; enter your own heart; learn to know your own soul. Examine who you are and who you have been; what you should be and what you should do, what you were by nature and what you are now through sin; what you should have been through diligence and what you still can be through grace." (*Treatise on the Interior House*, c. 36, n. 76; PL 184, 545.) Likewise, Richard of St. Victor, *The Mystical Ark*, III, c. 6 (PL 196, 116–17) offers another source: "He who does not know himself cannot rightly estimate the worth of anything. He who does not consider the worth of his original condition does not know how all earthly pride should lie under his feet. He who does not first reflect upon his spirit knows nothing, and he does not know what he ought to think concerning the angelic spirit or the divine Spirit. If you are not able to enter into yourself, how will you be capable of examining those things which are within or above you? If you are not worthy to enter into the first tabernacle, with what impudence do you dare to enter into the second tabernacle, that is, into the Holy of Holies? If you are not able to struggle along the high paths so that with the Lord Jesus or at least with Moses you can ascend into a high mountain, with what impudence

do you come forth to fly to the heavens? First return to yourself; then you may dare to examine those things which are above you."

90 Cf. Exodus 26, 34–35.

91 Saint Bonaventure refers to three sections of the temple: 1) the outer court, atrium, or vestibule; 2) the Sanctuary, the Holy place, the anterior part of the Tabernacle, or first Tabernacle; 3) the Holy of Holies, or the second Tabernacle. The outer court or vestibule corresponds to the first two steps of the *Itinerarium* and is an analogy of the world. The Sanctuary or anterior part of the Tabernacle corresponds to the third and fourth steps of the *Itinerarium* and is an analogy of the mind. The Holy of Holies corresponds to the fifth and sixth steps of the *Itinerarium* and is an analogy of God.

92 Cf. Psalm 4, 6: "Let the light of your face shine on us, O Lord!"

93 *image.* Saint Bonaventure in his *Commentary on Book I of the Sentences*, d. 3, p. 2, a. 1, qq. 1–3 (I, 80–87), employs his favorite analogy (memory, intelligence, and will), borrowed from Saint Augustine's *On the Trinity*, to show why the mind is called an image of God.

Saint Augustine, in *On the Trinity*, XIV, c. 8 (PL 42, 1044), says: "Although the human mind is not of the same nature as God, still the image of that nature which is greater than every other is to be sought and discovered in that part of our nature that is greater than every other part, namely in our mind. In the mind itself, even before it participates in God, there is an image of Him. For, even though the mind, having lost its participation in God, is deformed, it still remains an image of God. Since the mind has a capacity for God and can participate in God, by that very fact it is His image. In fact, it has this lofty end precisely because it is His image.

Thus, we have here the mind remembering itself, understanding itself, loving itself. Seeing this, we perceive in it a trinity—a trinity far less than God, but nonetheless an image of God."

Augustine, here, is simply unfolding the discussion he has held earlier in *On the Trinity*, X, c. 11 (PL 42, 983–84): "Setting aside for a short time all the other things of which the mind is certain concerning itself, let us consider and discuss in particular the following three powers: memory, understanding, and will."

In discussing memory, understanding, and will in his *Commentary on Book I of the Sentences*, Saint Bonaventure sees the relation of these powers to the mind in a way parallel to the relation of the three Persons to the divine essence. The soul as image of the Trinity will be interpreted in a way consistent with the Christian belief in the Trinity. As there is only one God and yet the three Persons are really distinct Persons, so the mind, the image of the Trinity, is one mind with three powers that are not independent substances. Yet these powers are not simply modes or qualities of the mind any more than the three Persons are modes of the divine essence. To express this, Saint Bonaventure says that these three powers (memory, understanding, and will) are more than qualities; they are substances, but not independent substances, since this would make the soul an image of tritheism. Bonaventure claims that these three powers are substances by reduction (i.e. they lean more toward substances than toward accidents).

94 *not with your bodily eye, but with the eye of your mind.* In his *Breviloquium*, II, c. 12 (V, 230), Saint Bonaventure claims to follow Hugh of St. Victor (*On the Sacraments of the Christian Faith*, I, p. 10, c. 2; ed. Roy J. Deferrari, 167; PL 176, 329–30) in assigning a threefold vision to man: "the eye of the flesh, the eye of reason, and the eye of contemplation. The eye of the flesh that he might see the world and the things contained in the world; the eye of reason that he might see the soul and the things contained in the soul; and the eye of contemplation that he might see God and the things contained in God. And so by the bodily eye man would see the things outside him; by the eye of reason he would see the things within him; and by the eye of contemplation he would see the things above him."

95 *memory.* This term has a much wider scope than it usually has in modern usage. Saint Bonaventure follows Saint Augustine closely as he speaks of memory's three main meanings.

The first activity of memory concerns the retention and the representation of internal and external experiences, including the past, the present, and the future. In the *Disputed Questions on the Mystery of the Trinity* (q. 5, a. 1; V, 90) Saint Bonaventure shows more fully the reflections of God's eternity in the activity of memory: "In the soul, which is the image of God, there is memory of past things, understanding of present things, and foreknowledge of future things. And these things are present in the soul simultaneously, so that in the soul, which is a spiritual substance, at one moment are gathered together and conjoined things which follow one after the other in time. However, since the soul itself is limited and gets its knowledge of these successive things from things outside, this simultaneity is distinct from that perfect simultaneity [which is the eternity of God]."

The second activity of memory concerns the retention and representation of simple geometrical, physical, or mathematical principles, such as a point, an instant, or a unit, that are the bases of any continuous or discrete quantities. Such basic principles are not rooted in sense experience and have their ruling or measuring authority from above. Ultimately they lead us to God as the Eternal Art and Measure of all here below. See above, n. 80.

The third activity of memory concerns the first principles and axioms of the sciences. These are principles that cannot be totally based on sense experience. They are principles, like "The whole is greater than any part," that cannot be erased from the memory. We cannot even think of it as being not true. This activity of memory thus reveals that in the soul there is a changeless light in which it recalls the changeless Truth that is God. Thus, through these principles we already possess the changeless Truth in our souls.

96 *axioms.* Aristotle, in his *Posterior Analytics*, tells us that we cannot prove everything by a formal argument. A conclusion of an argument is always based

on premises or starting points. Those premises may themselves have been proven conclusions from a preceding argument. We could keep going back to how each premise was proved, but ultimately we must get back to a premise that itself was not proved and is self-evident. Such self-evident premises are what Aristotle calls axioms or dignities, since they must be given a place of honor. They are principles that are clear to all, such as "The same thing cannot be and not be at the same time under the same aspect."

97 Aristotle, *Posterior Analytics* 1, 7 (75a 42) and 1, 10 (76b 14).

98 See Saint Augustine, *On the Trinity*, XIV, c. 8, n. 11, quoted above in n. 93.

99 The position of Saint Bonaventure is that a full analysis or understanding of the term 'being' cannot be attained unless we go back to complete and absolute Being or God. God, then, is the first thing known even though we are not conscious of it. Only when we analyze what we know do we come to realize that God is the ground of all being and all understanding. There is, despite the fact that God is the first thing known, still need for proofs for the existence of God. On this matter, see Etienne Gilson, *The Philosophy of St. Bonaventure*, c. 3: "The Evidence for God's Existence," 107–26. See above, note 80.

Saint Bonaventure's *Disputed Questions on the Mystery of the Trinity* (*Quaestiones disputatae de mysterio Trinitatis*), q. 1 (V, 46–47) provides arguments that serve as explicit commentaries on the present section of the *Itinerarium*. As a help in following the order of the *Itinerarium*, we adapt the order of the *Disputed Questions on the Mystery of the Trinity* (tr. Zachary Hayes; St. Bonaventure, N.Y.: Franciscan Institute Publications 1979, 110–11) to the order of the *Itinerarium*:

[15]. "If there is diminished being or qualified being, there is a being that exists absolutely, because qualified being can neither exist nor be understood unless it is understood through unqualified being. Neither can diminished being exist or be understood except through perfect being, just as a privation cannot be understood except with respect to a habit. Therefore, if every created being is being only in part, and if the uncreated being alone is absolute and perfect being, it is necessary that any category of being implies and leads to the conclusion that God exists.

[18]. "Again, if there is being in potency, there is being in act, because a potency can be reduced to act only through a being in act, and there would be no potency unless it were capable of being reduced to act. If that being which is pure act and has no potency is none other than God, it is necessary that everything other than the first being implies the fact that God exists.

[12]. "Again, if there is being that exists from another, there is also being that does not exist from another, because nothing can bring itself from nonbeing to being. Therefore, there must necessarily be a first principle of eduction, and this is found in the first being which is not educed from another. Therefore, if that being which exists from another is called a created being, and that being

which does not exist from another is called uncreated being—and this is God, then every category of being implies the existence of God.

[14]. "Again, if there is relative being, there is also absolute being, because the relative is never terminated except in the absolute. But an absolute being which depends on no other can only be a being that receives nothing from another. This is the first being, and all other being is in some way dependent. Therefore it is necessary that every category of being implies the existence of God.

[11]. "[Again], if there is posterior being, then there is prior being, because there is nothing posterior except it be from something prior. But if the sum total of posterior being exists, there must necessarily be a first being. Therefore, if it is necessary to say that among creatures there is both posterior and prior, it is necessary that the sum total of creatures implies and cries out that there is a first principle.

[20]. "Again, if there is changeable being, there is also unchangeable being, since—as the Philosopher proves—movement takes its origin from a being at rest and terminates in a being at rest. If, therefore, that being which is entirely unchangeable is none other than the first being—which is God—and if all others are created, and insofar as they are created, they are changeable, it is necessary that the existence of God is implied by any category of being.

[19]. "Again, if there is composite being, there is simple being, because a composite does not have being of itself. Therefore, it is necessary that it take its origin from something that is simple. But the most simple being, having no trace of composition, is none other than the first being. Therefore, every other being implies God."

100 Averroes, *On the Soul*, III, c. 6, t. 25 (ed. F. S. Crawford, 462), where the text reads: "Generally privations are known only through contraries, namely through a knowledge of a quality and its privation. And Aristotle meant here (430b 24) that we know blackness as a privation of whiteness."

101 John 1, 1 and 1, 9. On the illumination theory see n. 80 and Etienne Gilson, *The Philosophy of St. Bonaventure*, c. XII: "The Illumination of the Intellect," 309–64.

102 Augustine, *On True Religion*, 39, 72 (PL 34, 154): "Do not go outside. Return within yourself, for truth dwells in the interior man. If you find that your interior nature is mutable, then transcend yourself. But remember that when you transcend yourself, you must even transcend yourself as a reasoning soul. Head for the place where the light itself of reason gets its light. To what does every good reasoning person go, except to the truth? Still truth is not attained by reasoning, but it is that which is the goal of all who reason."

103 The notion of the highest good. See Saint Augustine, *On the Trinity*, VIII, 3, 4 (PL 42, 949): "Only what is good draws your love. The earth . . . , the beautiful and fertile earth . . . , a human face with its balanced features, its happy smile, its rich coloring . . . , the heart of a friend. . . . But enough! There is this good, and there is that good. Take away the 'this' and 'that' and

look, if you can, upon the good itself. Then you will behold God, Who is not good because He has the good of any other good thing but because He is the good of every good thing. . . . So, our love should rise to God as the Good itself."

104 *desire.* Saint Bonaventure's *Disputed Questions on the Mystery of the Trinity*, 1, 7 (V, 46; tr. Zachary Hayes, 109), in the form of a proof for the existence of God, provides a commentary on the meaning of 'desire': "The desire for happiness is implanted in us in such a way that no one can doubt that other men wish to be happy, as Augustine writes in many places. But happiness is found in the highest good, which is God. Therefore, if such desire is impossible without some knowledge, it is necessary that the knowledge by which we know the existence of God as the highest good be implanted in the soul itself." Cf. Augustine, *On the Trinity*, XIII, cc. 3–9, nn. 6–11 (PL 42, 1017–23) and also Boethius, *The Consolation of Philosophy*, III (PL 63, 719–86; tr. S. J. Tester, Cambridge: Harvard University Press [Loeb Classical Library, v. 74], 1973, 229–311).

105 *mental word.* Saint Bonaventure, in his *Commentary on Book I of the Sentences*, d. 27, p. 2, q. 1, a. 3 (I, 487–88), traces his explanation of 'mental word' to Saint Anselm's *Monologium*, c. 33 (ed. F. S. Schmitt, I, 52; tr. S. N. Deane, LaSalle, Illinois: Open Court Publishing Company, 1962, 96–97): "When I think of a man who is now absent, my mind focuses on the kind of image I have of him in my memory and that I gained by my sight of him. This image that exists in my mind when I think of him I call a mental word or image of the same man. The rational mind, then, when it understands itself by thinking of itself, has along with itself an image of itself born of itself, that is, it has a thought of itself that is a likeness of itself, formed in its likeness as it were by an impression of it. Now this image is its mental word. Who, then, can deny that the supreme Wisdom, when it understands itself by expressing itself, begets a likeness of itself consubstantial with it, namely, its Word?" Following this description of Saint Anselm, Saint Bonaventure then concludes: "A 'mental word' is nothing but an expressed and expressive likeness conceived by the power of the understanding mind and by means of which it perceives itself or something else." For Saint Augustine, a 'mental word,' in contrast with a written or spoken one, is "one that belongs to no particular language." See Augustine, *On the Trinity*, XV, c. 10, n. 19; c. 12, n. 22; and c. 27, n. 50 (PL 42, 1071, 1075, 1097). On the source of Saint Anselm's citation see Saint Augustine, *On the Trinity*, IX, c. 11 (PL 42, 969–70).

106 *word.* There is an analogy or parallel for Saint Bonaventure, following Saint Augustine and Anselm, between different elements connected with our knowing and the Trinity of persons in God. See above, n. 93. Saint Bonaventure will examine the doctrine of the Trinity to understand better the nature and operations of human knowing, and he will also examine human knowledge to come to a fuller understanding of the Trinity. As he says in the *Sermons on the Six Days of Creation*, III, 4 (V, 343): "It is impossible for the highest Spirit

that it not understand itself; and since that which is understood when it understands itself is equal to that which understands, that which understands grasps all that is and all that can be. Therefore, that which is understood is equal to the one understanding and is its likeness. This likeness is the Word, because, according to Augustine and Anselm, the likeness of a mind that focuses on itself, a likeness that exists in the highest region of the mind, is a *word*. Therefore, if this likeness is equal to God, it is God; and originating from God, it represents the originator and whatever the Father is able to create; therefore it represents many things." See A. Gerken, "Der johanneische Ansatz in der Christologie des hl. Bonaventura" in *Wissenschaft und Weisheit* 27 (1964), 89–100 and Z. Hayes, *What Manner of Man? Sermons on Christ by St. Bonaventure*, 76–79, nn. 4, 5, 8, 11.

107 Circumincession is the perfect being-in-one-another of the divine Persons in spite of their distinction as Persons. As Saint Bonaventure says in his *Commentary on Book I of the Sentences*, d. 19, p. 1, q. 1, a. 4 (I, 349): "Circumincession is that by which something is said to exist in another and vice versa. This properly and perfectly is found in God alone, because circumincession simultaneously implies in being both a distinction and a unity. Now, since in God alone is there the highest unity along with true distinction, so that distinction is not blunted and unity is not compromised, it follows that in God alone is perfect circumincession."

108 *cause of being, . . . basis of understanding, . . . ordering of our life.* See Saint Augustine, who, in *The City of God*, VIII, c. 4 (PL 41, 228), attributes this threefold truth concerning God to Plato: "This perhaps may be said of Plato's best disciples—that is, of those who followed most closely and understood most clearly the teachings of a master who has been rightly esteemed above all other pagan philosophers—that, at least, they sensed these truths about God: that in Him is to be found the cause of being, the basis of understanding, and the ordering of life. The first of these truths belongs to natural philosophy; the second to rational philosophy; the third to moral philosophy."

109 In regard to the division of sciences, see the somewhat longer explanation in *The Reduction of Arts to Theology*, c. 4 (V, 320–21; tr. Emma Thérèse Healy; Saint Bonaventure, N.Y.: Franciscan Institute Publications, 1955, 25–27).

110 Psalm 75, 5.

Chapter Four

111 Isaiah 24, 20.
112 Cf. Psalm 36, 4.
113 John 10, 9.
114 I Timothy 2, 5; cf. Genesis 2, 9.
115 See Saint Bonaventure, *Commentary on Book I of the Sentences*, d. 3, p. 2, a. 2, q. 1: "Properly speaking an image consists in a unity of essence and

a trinity of powers, and according to this unity and trinity the soul is capable of being sealed by that most high Trinity with an image of likeness, and this consists in grace and the theological virtues." In *The Breviloquium*, V, 4 (V, 256) he adds: "Again, since perfect rectitude of the soul requires that the soul be rectified according to both its superior and inferior aspect, . . . therefore it is necessary that in regard to its superior aspect, where the soul is an image of the Trinity, that it be rectified through the three theological virtues, so that just as the image of creation consists in the trinity of powers with the unity of essence, so the image of redemption will consist in the trinity of habits with the unity of grace. For, it is by these habits that the soul is carried directly to the supreme Trinity in a way that corresponds to the appropriated attributes of the three Persons: faith, through belief and assent, leads to the supreme Truth; hope, through trust and expectation, leads to the loftiest Height; and charity, through desire and love, leads to the greatest Good."

116 Galatians 4, 26.

117 John 14, 6.

118 Hebrews 1, 3; cf. John 1, 1.

119 *spiritual hearing and sight.* The supernatural power of grace gives to the human soul something like new powers for the understanding of immediate experience. Through its activity the influence of the Holy Spirit is perfected in a loving understanding of God and a dedication to Him. These powers are the spiritual senses, analogous to the five external senses. Through them the human mind, in a manner corresponding to its new life, becomes immediately present to the life-giving activity of divine grace. The soul, in a way analogous to the experiences of the external senses, now sees, hears, smells, tastes, and feels differently. Saint Bonaventure, here in section 3, gives examples of each sense. Thus, through the supernatural power of grace in the human soul, the highest spiritual joy that is possible in this present state of pilgrimage reaches its perfection through immediate, spiritual experiences analogous to sense experiences.

In *The Breviloquium*, V, 6 (V, 259), Saint Bonaventure indicates that the five spiritual senses do not represent new habits, but rather represent states of delight and enjoyment of spiritual perceptions filling and consoling the souls of just men. "The spiritual senses express mental graspings of the Truth that is contemplated. Now this contemplation was given to the prophets through revelation according to the three modes of seeing: the sensorial, the imaginative, and the intellective, while other just men obtain it through speculation that starts from the senses, reaches the imagination, proceeds from the imagination to reason, from reason to understanding, from understanding to intelligence, and from intelligence to wisdom, which is an ecstatic knowledge that begins in this life and reaches fulfillment in eternal glory. Of such successive steps is Jacob's ladder made, with its top reaching to heaven; and thus also is the throne of Solomon made, upon which is seated the King most wise, truly peaceful, and full of love. . . ."

120 Cf. Apocalypse 2, 17.

121 Canticle of Canticles 3, 6; 6, 9; 8, 5.

122 *hierarchical*. The prologue of Saint Bonaventure's *The Triple Way* (*De triplici via*; VIII, 3) establishes the hierarchy of which Saint Bonaventure speaks here: "purgation, illumination, and perfective union. Purgation leads to peace, illumination to truth, and perfective union to love. As soon as the soul has mastered these three, it becomes holy, and its merits increase in the measure of its completion of them, for upon the proper understanding of these three states are founded both the understanding of all Scripture and the meriting of eternal life." *The Triple Way* details this threefold hierarchy, especially in its first chapter.

123 Apocalypse 21, 2.

124 Bernard of Clairvaux, *On Consideration* V, 12 (*Sancti Bernardi Opera*, t. 3; edd. J. Leclercq and H. M. Rochais; Rome, 1963), 476–77: "God loves as Charity, He knows as Truth, He sits in judgment as Equity, He prevails as Majesty, He rules as Power, He guards as Salvation, He acts as Strength, He reveals as Light, and He assists as Kindness. And these things also the angels do. . . ."

125 I Corinthians 15, 28.

126 I Timothy 1, 5; cf. Romans 13, 10.

127 Matthew 22, 40.

128 Apocalypse 1, 8; 21, 6; 22, 13.

129 Saint Bonaventure, in the prologue of *The Breviloquium* (V, 204–5), comments on the words of Saint Paul's Letter to the Ephesians 3, 18 that speak of 'the breadth and length and height and depth of Christ's love' that is revealed in the sacred Scriptures. In dealing with the height of the Scriptures, he declares: "Height, also, is found in the Scriptures as they unfold. It is seen in the description of the hierarchies and of their ordered ranks, the ecclesiastical, the angelic, and the divine. . . . Eternal Wisdom uses philosophical knowledge as its servant, borrowing from the natural order what it needs to make a mirror for the representation of things divine; erecting, as it were, a ladder, whose foot rests upon the earth but whose top reaches heaven. And all this is done through the one Hierarch, Jesus Christ, who is Hierarch not only in the hierarchy of the Church by reason of the human nature He assumed, but also in the angelic hierarchy, and again, as the Second Person, sharing the supercelestial hierarchy of the most blessed Trinity."

130 Psalm 109, 3.

131 Cf. Psalm 4, 9.

132 Cf. Canticle of Canticles 2, 7.

133 Cf. Isaiah 6, 2.

134 Galatians 3, 19.

135 Romans 5, 5.

136 I Corinthians 2, 11.

137 Cf. Ephesians 3, 18–19.

Chapter Five

138 Psalm 4, 7.

139 Augustine, *Eighty-Three Questions*, q. 51, n. 4 (PL 40, 33): "There are some who wish that the mind be made an image, for the mind is formed by Truth itself without any intervening substance."

140 Cf. Exodus 25, 1–39.

141 Cf. Exodus 3, 14.

142 *Ibid.*

143 Matthew 28, 19.

144 Luke 18, 19.

145 John Damascene, *On the Orthodox Faith*, I, 9, 142 (PG 94, 835–36): "It seems that of all the names predicated of God the more proper name is 'He Who Is,' since when He spoke to Moses on the mountain, He said: Say to the children of Israel 'He Who Is' has sent me."; Pseudo-Dionysius, *On the Divine Names*, III, 1 (PG 3, 679–80): "And first of all, if it pleases you, let us consider the name 'The Good.' This is a perfect name, since it manifests all the emanations of God."

146 Saint Bonaventure, in his *Commentary on Book I of the Sentences*, d. 8, p. 1, q. 1, a. 2 (I, 154), states: "So great is the truth of divine being that you cannot judge it not to exist unless there is something wrong with your understanding, so that you do not know what is meant by 'God.' There cannot be anything wrong on the side of the object to be understood, since there cannot be on its part a lack of presence or evidence, considering God in Himself or as the object of a proof of His existence."

147 On how we are to understand that God is the first thing known, see above, nn. 80 and 95.

148 *Ibid.*

149 Aristotle, *Metaphysics*, II, c. 1, t. 1 (993b 9–11).

150 Cf. Psalm 138, 11.

151 *Behold, if you can, this most pure Being.* From all that has been said about the theory of illumination (nn. 80 and 95) and the indubitability of the existence of God (nn. 80 and 99), it is obvious that the 'reasons' or proofs which Saint Bonaventure offers for the existence of God, insofar as they imply the existence of God, are not considered by him as proofs or reasons which first make known the existence of God, since the existence of God is evident in itself and is immediately known in the proposition 'God exists.' Hence, the reasons taken from the exterior world, although not denied by Saint Bonaventure, are not of primary importance; they are rather stimuli inducing us to think and to become aware of the immediacy of our cognition of God. The being perceived in any created being cannot be perceived in its ultimate meaning without the knowledge of the Being which is God. Neither can any absolute and final and evident truth be known with certitude without the divine light shining through the objects and ideas. This light is always there; we have but to pay full attention

to it. When we bring to full awareness the content of our first idea, it is impossible for us to think that God does not exist.

The knowledge of God, for Saint Bonaventure, is immediately given to us, not in a vision of His essence, but in the impossibility of the denial of His existence, as soon as the proposition "God exists" is formulated and understood correctly, for the existence of God is included in the notion of God. We may deny His existence, but the denial is not evident and cannot be evident. We may believe that we do not know God, because we are ignorant of the meaning of the term 'God,' but if we go to the bottom of our knowledge and conceive God as 'being itself,' there is no possibility of giving our assent to the denial of His existence. See Etienne Gilson, *The Philosophy of Saint Bonaventure*, c. 3: "The Evidence for God's Existence," 107–26.

152 See Saint Bonaventure, *Disputed Questions on the Mystery of the Trinity*, q. 3, a. 1, response 7 (V, 72), where he argues that there is no diversity on the part of God, but that if there is diversity it is due to our different ways of understanding God.

153 *most actual.* That is, Pure Act. This is a philosophical term corresponding to the Biblical 'He Who Is.'

154 Aristotle, *Topics* V, c. 3 (134b 23–24).

155 Deuteronomy 6, 4.

156 Saint Bonaventure, in his *Commentary on Book I of the Sentences*, d. 2, a. 1, q. 4, doubt I, indicates that "the mind, if it is going to contemplate God perfectly, needs to be purified both in regard to the intellect and in regard to the will." He then notes that the intellect is purified through faith and the will is purified through justice.

157 Apocalypse 1, 8; cf. Proverbs 16, 4.

158 Alan of Lille, *Theological Rules*, n. 7 (PL 210, 627): "God is an intelligible sphere whose center is everywhere and whose circumference is nowhere." At the end of his explanation of rule 7 he notes that "God is one Who while remaining stable makes all things move." See n. 159.

159 Boethius, *Consolation of Philosophy*, III, meter 9, provides in verse (*"Stabilisque manens das cuncta moveri"*—"And remaining still, grant motion to all else") the explanation given less poetically by Alan of Lille in his commentary on Rule 7. See n. 158.

160 I Corinthians 15, 28.

161 Romans 11, 36.

162 Exodus 33, 19.

Chapter Six

163 Cf. Exodus 25, 19.

164 This is the peak of Saint Bonaventure's philosophical speculations as a help to the return of the mind to God. The immediacy of the knowledge of the necessity of God's existence which is given to everyone who fully resolves

his ideas, especially the idea of being, is still more accentuated in the act of contemplation which is proper to the fifth stage. Now the soul, its gaze fixed on the idea of being, freely turns from the one attribute of God's being to another, perceiving their intimate connection and interrelation, enraptured and full of admiration. When it now passes to the idea of Goodness, revealed by Sacred Scripture, the soul climbs a step higher to the highest peak toward which contemplative theology tends, and contemplates the necessity of the generation and spiration of the Blessed Trinity itself. Now there is nothing left to the soul but the rest of the seventh day.

165 Pseudo-Dionysius, *The Heavenly Hierarchy*, 4 (PG 3, 181–82): "The Good ... offers through its very being its goodness to all beings." On the great influence of Pseudo-Dionysius on St. Bonaventure's view of the Trinity and on this chapter of the *Itinerarium*, see Zachary Hayes's introduction to Saint Bonaventure, *Disputed Questions on the Mystery of the Trinity* (St. Bonaventure, N.Y., 1979), 22–25.

166 Saint Bonaventure is not claiming here the possibility of proving the Trinity by natural reason, but merely of indicating proofs of fittingness. The necessity he speaks of in regard to these proofs is the 'necessity of suitableness.'

167 See above, n. 145. The position indicated in note 145 is also found in Saint Bonaventure, *Commentary on Book I of the Sentences*, d. 22, q. 1, a. 3 (I, 395): "If we speak of the names that God has given to Himself when He has understood Himself in a proper sense, then the names of this type are proper names. Such are said to be the names 'Good' and 'He Who Is.' Wherefore, Dionysius seems to want that the name 'Good' alone is proper to God and His principal name. Damascenus, on the other hand, seems to want that the name 'He Who Is' alone is proper to God and His principal name."

168 Exodus 25, 20.

169 John 17, 3.

170 Genesis 1, 26.

171 Saint Bonaventure, in *The Breviloquium*, I, 3 (V, 212), explains: "Likewise, since the Son is image, He is also Word and Son. Image designates Him as the expressed likeness; Word designates Him as the expressive likeness, and Son designates Him as the hypostatic likeness." See above, n. 106.

Chapter Seven

172 *heavenly wisdom*. Saint Bonaventure follows Saint Augustine and makes wisdom in the Christian sense the ideal of man's search for knowledge and ultimate peace. What is wisdom? Saint Bonaventure uses this term in many meanings. It is necessary to distinguish them if one wishes to understand correctly those texts where Saint Bonaventure uses this term. Wisdom can be understood in four different senses:

1) The first is 'wisdom' in the ordinary or common understanding of the term. It means a general knowledge of things. In this broad sense, Saint

Augustine uses it to mean the knowledge of things divine and human. In this sense, we can identify wisdom with a broad general knowledge.

2) The second sense of 'wisdom' is a less common sense. It means not a general knowledge, but a sublime one, for it is the knowledge of eternal things. Thus, wisdom is distinguished from science, which is the knowledge of created things according to Saint Augustine. Saint Bonaventure will also understand Aristotle to use 'wisdom' in this second sense when he calls it the knowledge of the highest causes. In this sense we can identify wisdom with first philosophy or metaphysics.

3) The third sense of 'wisdom' is the proper sense: it means the knowledge of God that is accompanied by piety, that is, a knowledge of God attained in worshipping Him by faith, hope, and charity. Saint Augustine understands wisdom in this sense when he explains the words of Holy Scripture (Job 28, 28): "Behold, wisdom is piety itself." Thus, Bonaventure can identify 'wisdom' with true religion, that is, a truly Christian life.

4) The fourth sense of 'wisdom' is a more strict sense of the term. It means 'experiential knowledge of God.' In this sense, 'wisdom' is one of the gifts of the Holy Spirit. An act flowing from this gift or divinely given habit is an act of tasting the sweetness of God. This wisdom truly pertains to the mystical state; it begins in knowledge and ends in affection, and has no limits as to its intensity.

'Wisdom' in this last sense is the goal of Saint Bonaventure's life and work. He calls it 'peace' here in the *Itinerarium* (Prologue, 1 and VII, 1). He calls it 'a certain learned ignorance' in *The Breviloquium* V, 6 (V, 260). He calls it 'charity' (*Reduction of the Arts to Theology*, 26; V, 260). All these names mean to him one and the same thing, the real goal of man here upon earth: the wisdom of mystical union with God that is a knowledge by tasting. See above, n. 21.

If the highest wisdom here upon earth is obtainable only in mystical union with God, why then should one care about scientific activity with its heavy burden of methodical thinking and its detours of reasoning? Is not the straightest way to it found in the the way of Saint Francis, loving God in all simplicity, stripping oneself of all earthly things and affections in order to be free to fly away to the union of love with God without any special intellectual culture?

Saint Bonaventure pays his unrestricted respect to this way, but he does not choose it for himself or for the audience to whom he speaks. For that path can be travelled only if a special vocation is given. Saint Bonaventure and the students to whom he addresses himself have another way to attain this ideal of contemplation, namely, in that wisdom which is contemplative or mystical union. For Saint Bonaventure's vocation, and that of his audience, is that of the theologian who craves union through understanding. In his *Sermons on the Six Days of Creation*, 17, 6 (V, 410), he declares: "As the body without food loses its strength, beauty, and health, so the soul without understanding of the truth becomes dismal and weak, and deformed and miserable in all things. Therefore, it needs to be fed."

Saint Bonaventure gives us the program of a theologian who has imbued the spirit of Saint Francis. He himself has truly lived up to this program. The ultimate aim of this work and of all his works is not so much to cultivate the intellect as, by cultivating the intellect, to lead his listeners and readers to the main goal, which is union with God in true wisdom. Though this goal is more or less visible in every writing which came from his pen, it has found its most clear expression in the *Itinerarium*, in *The Reduction of the Arts to Theology*, and in the *Sermons on the Six Days of Creation*. In these works, in particular, he puts speculation and all the sciences into the service of the ultimate goal, which is the mystical union with God.

In *The Reduction of the Arts to Theology*, 26 (V, 325), Saint Bonaventure makes clear the connections of all sciences and skills with theology, and through theology with mystical union with God. There he concludes: "And this is the fruit of all sciences, that in all of them, faith may be strengthened, God may be honored, character may be formed, and consolation may be derived from union of the Spouse with His beloved, a union that takes place through charity, to the attainment of which the whole purpose of sacred Scripture, and consequently, every illumination descending from above, is directed. And this charity is that without which all knowledge is vain, because no one comes to the Son except through the Holy Spirit Who teaches us all the truth and Who is blessed forever."

Thus, by vivifying all knowledge and all human endeavor and research with the spirit of love, the tension experienced by every intellectual mystic is relaxed. All one-sidedness of intellectual and scientific activity is out-balanced, or absorbed, as it were, by the other activity which culminates in charity. The manner of speculation that Saint Bonaventure has in mind is beautifully expressed to the readers of the *Itinerarium* in Prologue, 4. It is through the fruitful marriage of speculation and charity, science and wisdom, intellectual search and mysticism that Saint Bonaventure has met the challenge of the intellectual vocation within the Franciscan order that he and the theologians inspired by Saint Francis had to meet.

173 I Timothy 2, 5.

174 John 14, 6 and 10, 7.

175 Exodus 25, 20; Ephesians 3, 9. What preceded was not vision. It was an awareness of something divine. It was an obscured knowledge in which the divine reality was seen but only through the foggy mirror of created things and the human expressions found in divine revelation. The direct and full contact with the divine reality, however, is possible to us through grace in Christ, if we leave behind the 'clarity' of the intellect and through love plunge into the depths of the Divine Ocean. For love reaches further than vision.

176 Exodus 12, 11.

177 Apocalypse 2, 17.

178 Luke 23, 43.

179 Genesis 35, 10.

180 Saint Bonaventure, in explaining the role played by the eternal ideas
in our knowledge, always repeats the observation that the ideas act as the
motives and controlling reasons in our knowledge. What is meant by this? In
their function as controlling or regulating reasons, the ideas make our knowledge possible because they force the restless uncertainty and mutability of our
thought under an unrelenting law. It is, therefore, the very immutability of the
divine Truth, which, though dimly seen by our intellect, gives to our knowledge
the transcendent characteristics of necessity, immutability, eternity, and abso-
luteness. The eye of our mind is pointed by this faintly perceived light in the
right direction, as the eye of a helmsman is guided by a dim light on a dark
night. Hence, Saint Bonaventure, in the *Disputed Questions on the Knowledge
of Christ*, IV, 19 (V, 26), calls the eternal reasons 'guides.' For the same reason
the eternal ideas or rules are stimulating factors of our certain and final
knowledge.

The eternal ideas are also our motives: They are what move our minds.
Our inferior reason would be at a loss amid the multiplicity of our apprehensions
of created beings if the superior reason did not become aware of something
beyond the contingency of their being and if it were not moved toward the
eternal and immutable ideas, dimly shining forth through the veil of their
creatureliness. Only if we admit such a presence of the eternal rules and ideas
to the acts of our certain knowledge can we account for the fact that we are
able to grasp objects which transcend all creatures and our mind and are
common to all. They are present, but seen only faintly and in connection with
created beings. Hence, a direct vision of divine Truth or the divine essence
is foreign to Saint Bonaventure's doctrine. For he does not admit a direct
vision of divine Truth even in the mystical union of the soul with God, where
the soul, all its powers being united in the one act of love, embraces its God
in darkness. Therefore, Saint Bonaventure, in *The Breviloquium*, V, 6–7 (V,
260), calls this highest human experience a 'learned ignorance.' The light of
divine illumination or the ideas shine through the haze of creatures, remaining
remote from intuition. Hence we do not see the ideas in their purity, our eyes
being covered with a veil because of the obscurity that marks the mirror of
the soul which is the divine image. The eye of our mind cannot see them
without the interference of created things.

181 Apocalypse 2, 17.

182 Luke 12, 49.

183 I Corinthians 2, 10–11.

184 See above, n. 14.

185 Pseudo-Dionysius, *On Mystical Theology*, I, 1 (PG 3, 997–98): see above,
n. 25.

186 *superluminous darkness . . . resplendent above all splendor.* See Saint Bona-

venture, *Disputed Questions on the Knowledge of Christ*, 2, response 9 (V, 10): "That is why Saint Augustine frequently says that knowledge in the Word is like the light of day, but knowledge in its ordinary manner is like dusk, since every creature is darkness in relation to the divine light."

187 Isaiah 31, 9.

188 Job 7, 15.

189 Exodus 33, 20.

190 John 13, 1 and 14, 8; cf. II Corinthians 12, 9.

191 Psalm 72, 26 and 105, 48.